HISTORICAL BACKGROUND

'The fiercest serpent may be overcome by a swarm of ants.'

Admiral Yamamoto Isoroku speaking in opposition to the construction of the *Yamato* class battleships, expressing his belief that carrier-based aircraft could defeat the most powerful warships. (in *Scraps of Paper: The Disarmament Treaties Between the World Wars*, by H A Hyde, 1988)

Japan's present-day dynastic lines are traceable to the Emperor Jinmu-Tennō who ascended the throne in 660 BC. Over the next thousand years, the islands did not face any sustained overseas threats by sea until the arrival of the American naval commander Matthew Calbraith Perry in 1852 tasked by President Fillmore to forcibly open diplomatic relations with the Tokugawa shōgunate. This event marks the beginning of a profound change in Japanese thinking. With the recognition of the vulnerability of the country from the sea the shōgunate initiated an active policy of assimilation and adoption of Western naval technologies. Progress was rapid. The first steam warships were purchased in the 1850s, and organised naval training began at the same time, followed by building the first modern naval arsenals at Yokosuka (near Yokohama) and Nagasaki. Japan was still a country composed of domains governed by Daimyo, and interestingly the shōgunate allowed and encouraged each domain to develop their own naval fleets as each saw fit. This changed with the Boshin War that raged from 1868 to 1869. This revolutionary war wrested the control of Japan from the Tokugawa Shōgunate to the direct rule of the Emperor Meji and his Court, heralding the birth a national navy by amalgamating all the naval assets held by individual Daimyo.

In 1870 an Imperial decree determined that Britain's Royal Navy would serve as the model for naval development because both were island nations and the Royal Navy was the leading naval force of the age in terms of technology, innovation, and power. The British were willing to train the Japanese in order to make Japan an ally, avoiding a potential threat to Britain's widespread Asian colonies and extensive trading interests. In 1902 Japan formally became an ally of Great Britain under the Anglo-Japanese Alliance that required both nations to come to each other's aid if a war with more than two additional nations broke out. Under this close relationship Japanese shipbuilding developed rapidly, initially by building ships under foreign supervision, but there were already examples of home-grown technological innovation. From 1886 Japan manufactured her own prismatic gunpowder called Shimose Powder. Prismatic powder is based on picric acid that becomes unstable in contact with iron in shell casings. The British stabilized it by dilution with nitrobenzene and petroleum jelly to create Lyddite. The Shimose method coated the metal shell casing with unpigmented urushiol lacquer, a coating used for centuries to finish woodwork taken from the tree *Toxicodendron vernicifluum* that permitted undiluted powder to be packed into the casing, yielding a shell with greater heat and blast speed. The Japanese kept the method secret and applied it to mines, depth charges, and torpedo warheads. By the turn of the century, Japanese industrial capacity and construction experience grew rapidly and by 1918 there was no aspect of shipbuilding technology where Japanese capabilities fell significantly below the standards of other modern navies. Her yards had become as skilled and productive as any other culminating with the dreadnoughts *Fusō* in 1915 and *Yamashiro* in 1917.

Commodore Perry lands at Edo Bay to meet the representatives of Tokugawa Ieyoshi. *(Author's Collection)*

BATTLE EXPERIENCE

With rapid industrialization, Japan's need for natural resources grew. Japanese plan-

The battleship *Yamashiro* as completed in 1916. From *Japanese Naval Warship Photo Album: Battleships and Battle Cruisers*, edited by Kazushige Todaka. *(Author's Collection)*

ners viewed Qing China and her tributary states as a place to establish trading concessions like Western nations to exploit the vast resources required for Japanese industry. However, Qing China had recently purchased a new navy from German and British yards for the Beiyang Fleet led by Admiral Ding Ruchang. The Japanese saw this fleet in China's north as a major obstacle to their plans and in 1894 launched a war by invading Korea, then a Qing tributary. At the Battle of the Yellow Sea Vice-Admiral Itō Sukeyuki led the smaller Japanese fleet into battle.

The defeat of the Qing military garnered the Japanese extensive trading rights in China, and Japan was allowed to annex Korea and the island of Formosa (now Taiwan) as Japanese colonies. To the Western powers, Japan had emerged as an Asian challenge, particularly alarming Russia which led a campaign to contain Japanese ambitions, by pressuring Japan to return the strategically important Liaodong Peninsula in northeastern China. However, the return was viewed as a national humiliation, and the leadership of Japan initiated an aggressive build-up of all her military services in preparation for future confrontations.

This came in 1904 with the outbreak of the Russo-Japanese War. Japan considered Russia's presence in the Far East a constant threat, with command of the sea thwarted by the Russian naval squadrons at Port Arthur and Vladivostok. The early skirmishes were inconclusive, so the Russians decided to end the matter by sending the Baltic Fleet under the command of Admiral Zinovy Petrovich Rozhestvensky all the way to Port Arthur to join their Pacific Squadron with the intention to overwhelm and defeat the Japanese navy decisively. Despite having a large fleet, many of the Russian ships were obsolete, suffered from poor maintenance, and were manned with poorly trained crews. In May 1905 Rozhestvensky made for Vladivostok via the Tsushima Strait near Busan on Korea's southern coast. On the 27th, Admiral Tōgō Heihachirō's fleet was waiting and attacked in what became known as Tsushima or the Battle of the Japan Sea. The Japanese ships were superior in speed and armament, and over the course of the two-day battle, two-thirds of the Russian Fleet was sunk, six ships were captured, four reached the safety of Vladivostok, and six took refuge in neutral ports. The Japanese victory surprised the Western powers who had believed that the Russian fleet would be victorious. The Japanese credited victory to their more powerful Shimose powder, better training, the use of wireless telegraphy for communication – the first use of telegraphy in a naval engagement – and battle experience from the Sino-Japanese War.

JAPANESE NAVAL DEFENCE POLICY

Now a major navy with successful battle experience, the future development of the fleet required a naval policy to guide it. The naval theorist Admiral Satō Tetsu advocated a policy of preparing for potential conflict with the United States Navy despite the two countries having no major differences in foreign policy at the time. Satō adopted ideas from the American naval theoretician Alfred Thayer Mahan, who advocated decisive fleet actions and naval blockades. Satō argued that Japanese security was only guaranteed by a navy that could defeat the navy of the greatest hypothetical threat – and concluded that Japan's fleet should be at least 70% as strong as that of the United States.

Satō's conclusions were incorporated into the 1907 Imperial National Defence Plan that outlined a strategy that would attack the US battlefleet before it could reach the western Pacific, aiming for the gradual attrition of 10% to 20% of the American fleet, using submarines, land-based bombers, and light surface forces. They believed that the technical superiority

A licence-built Gloster Sparrowhawk flying off the dreadnought battleship *Yamashiro*'s turret in 1922. From *Japanese Naval Warship Photo Album: Battleships and Battle Cruisers*, edited by Kazushige Todaka. *(Author's Collection)*

of Japanese ships and the skill and determination of Japanese sailors would mitigate any disparity in firepower. The main battle fleet was to remain in home waters waiting for the approach of the Americans, reasoning that after a long transit to the Western Pacific and limited resupply, any American commander would be forced to commit in a single major battle decided by battleships in a line of battle akin to the Japanese tactics used by Admiral Tōgō at Tsushima. This strategy was known as the Decisive Battle Doctrine, and the expected location of the battle would be near the Ryukyu Island chain south of the Japanese home islands. However, as technology developed, the projected location moved eastward, moving to between the Bonin and the Mariana Islands during the mid-1920s to 1940. The Decisive Battle Doctrine required more capital ships and the Japanese embarked on building an 'Eight-Eight fleet', of eight modern battleships and eight battlecruisers, grounded on a theoretical USN strength of twenty-five battleships and heavy cruisers split between two oceans. The only barrier to building such a fleet was not technological inferiority but financial constraints and access to natural resources.

JAPANESE CARRIER AVIATION

Despite the adoption of the Decisive Battle Doctrine, in the 1930s advocates of the new submarine and naval aviation technologies anticipated the time for opposing fleets in line-of-battle was becoming obsolete, and these debates resulted in an indecisive approach to capital ship development. The navy closely monitored the development of combat aviation by Britain, France, and the United States during World War I, and in 1920 concluded that Britain was the most advanced. In 1921, at Japanese request, a British mission led by Captain William Forbes-Sempill of 27 members including pilots and engineers from British aircraft manufacturing firms travelled to Japan. The mission brought over one hundred naval aircraft comprising twenty different models to Lake Kasumigaura (located 60km from Tokyo). Japanese pilots trained on operational British aircraft such as the Gloster Sparrowhawk. The Japanese later ordered fifty of them and licence-built a further forty more at the Yokosuka Naval Arsenal. This experience provided impetus for the design and manufacture of domestically produced aircraft, beginning with the Mitsubishi 1MF designed by the British aircraft designer Herbert Smith. Sempill's mission also introduced the latest equipment, including torpedoes, bombs, machine guns, cameras, and communications gear. By the time the mission returned to Britain, the Japanese had acquired a sound foundation in aviation technology and began constructing a naval air arm, but the Japanese navy remained reliant on the British model for tactical and operational procedures. Notably, the mission provided drawings of the aircraft carriers *Argus* and *Hermes*, whose layout influenced *Hōshō*,

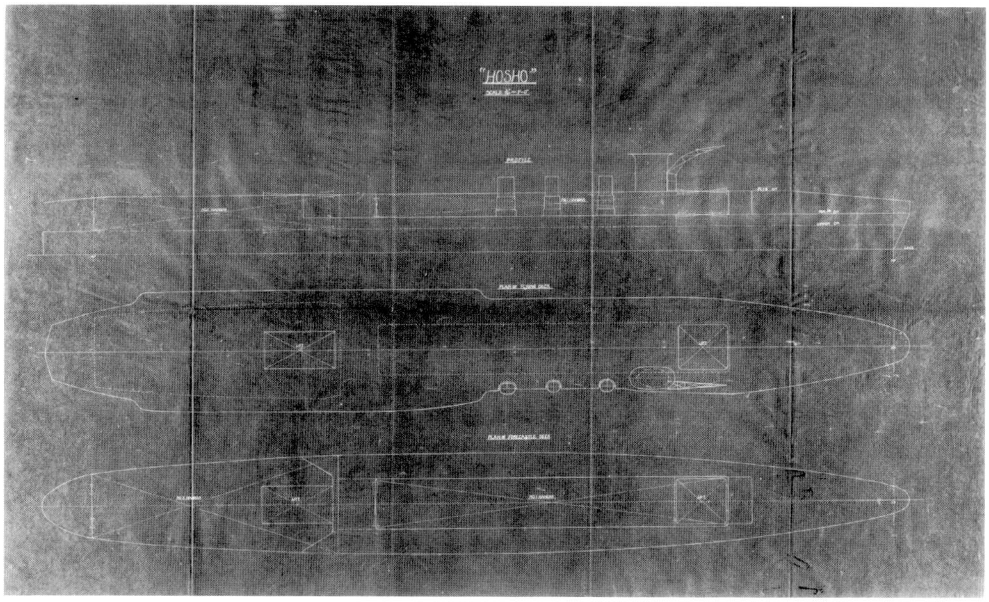

Hōshō's original design. *(University of Tokyo)*

the world's first purpose-built aircraft carrier. *Hōshō* was laid down in 1920 and commissioned in 1922, and used extensively for testing aircraft operations equipment, such as take-offs and landings, and carrier aircraft methods and tactics.

Hōshō's original design was as a seaplane carrier with a forward flying-off deck, island, funnels amidships, and a large hangar aft handling 32 aircraft. She was redesigned to include a rear deck to be able to land aircraft, modelled after the full deck fitted to *Furious* in 1918. She then had a small island and smoke was emitted from three funnels on her starboard side which hinged down to lie horizontal during flight operations. Unlike *Furious*, *Hōshō*'s flight deck was part of the ship's hull as a strength deck and not just superimposed on top of the ship's hull. In 1924, on the advice of aircrews to create an unobstructed full-length flight deck, her island was removed. The Japanese evaluated fifteen types of arresting gear finally settling on the British longitudinal wire system. At this time, naval aircraft were light weight and had low landing speeds, so the primary purpose of the gear was to prevent the aircraft from being blown over the side by sudden wind gusts. Japanese innovations included fitting a collapsible crane forward of the bridge for loading aircraft into the forward hangar, and a system of lights and mirrors along the flight deck assisted pilots in landing on the carrier as opposed to relying on batsmen guiding landing approaches. Her operational speed was 25 knots.

WASHINGTON NAVAL TREATY

In 1922 the Washington Naval Treaty (also known as the Five-Power Treaty) came into effect to prevent an arms race between the major naval powers by limiting warship construction. At the start of the conference, the American Secretary of State Charles Evans Hughes proposed a ten-year pause on the construction of battleships and battlecruisers, including the immediate

Hōshō conducting trials in Tokyo Bay in December 1922. From *Japanese Naval Warship Photo Album: Aircraft Carrier and Seaplane Carrier*, edited by Kazushige Todaka. *(Author's Collection)*

Kaga's battleship hull afloat. *(Author's Collection)*

suspension of capital ships under construction. Specifically, this meant the scrapping of existing or planned capital ships to produce a 5:5:3:1.67:1.67 ratio of tonnage for Britain, the United States, Japan, France, and Italy, respectively.

For the Japanese, the treaty would not allow a fleet 70 per cent the size of that of the United States required by the Decisive Battle Doctrine but they recognized that superior British and American industrial capacity in any lengthy war would inevitably end in defeat because gaining strategic parity was not economically possible. Moreover, Admiral Yamamoto Isoroku noted that the treaty did more to restrict the other parties than Japan. Despite this sound reasoning, acceptance of the treaty created serious dissatisfaction within the navy that climaxed on 29 December 1934, when formal notice was given that Japan would withdraw at the end of 1936; this was followed by a boycott of the Second London Naval Treaty designed to limit the growth in naval armaments until 1942.

THE GREAT KANTŌ EARTHQUAKE

Under the 8-8 Fleet Plan, two capital ships began construction in 1920. One was the *Kaga*, a *Tosa* class battleship, designed as an enlarged *Nagato* and laid down at the Kawasaki Yard in Kobe on 19 July 1920. After studying the performance of British capital ships at the Battle of Jutland in May 1916, the Japanese improved the *Nagato* design to incorporate better armour distribution to protect the main gun turrets and magazines, and thicker deck armour to protect against plunging fire. Existing mine and torpedo defences were also improved. However, the terms of the 1922 Washington Naval Treaty intervened and work on *Kaga* ceased on 5 February 1922.

The second ship was *Akagi*, laid down on 6 December 1920 at the Kure Navy Yard near Hiroshima as one of the four *Amagi* class battlecruisers for the 8-8 Fleet. The *Amagi* class was a lengthened version of the *Tosa* class but with a thinner armoured belt and deck, a more powerful propulsion system, and a modified secondary armament arrangement. On 16 December 1920, at Yokosuka Naval Yard near Yokohama, *Akagi*'s sister *Amagi* began construction. As for the *Tosa* class, the Washington Naval Treaty prevented the completion of the two ships, but the treaty did allow the suspended battleship and battlecruiser hulls to be converted into aircraft carriers up to a 27,000-ton limit. The design displacement of the *Amagi* class was 47,000 tons so meeting the treaty limitations would have been impossible. However, the Americans also had the same problem when designing a carrier conversion of their *Lexington* class battlecruisers, so a treaty exception (specifically Article IX) allowed the conversion of up to two capital ships under construction to 33,000-ton aircraft carriers. The *Akagi* and *Amagi* were selected for conversion.

On Saturday 1 September 1923, a

Surviving partial plan of *Amagi*'s intended conversion to an aircraft carrier illustrating the overhanging rear flight deck. *(University of Tokyo)*

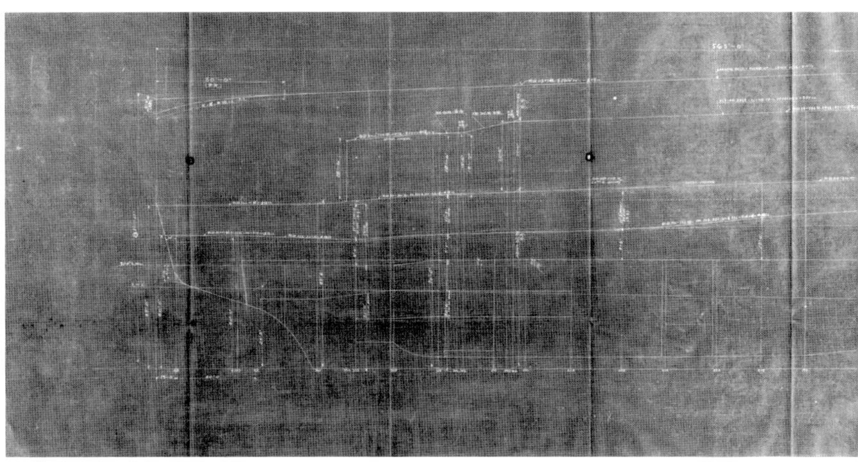

Kyogoku Kokugikan Sumo Stadium in Tokyo illustrated the destruction of the Great Kantō Earthquake of 1923. *(Great Kanto Earthquake Museum)*

massive earthquake measuring 7.9 to 8.2 on the magnitude scale (M_W – similar to the Richter Scale) shook the Kantō Plain. The Kantō Plain is the most extensive lowland (16,172 square km) on central Honshu that encompasses Tokyo and is the most productive and populous area of the country. The earthquake violently shook the area for between four and ten minutes depending on location, causing an estimated death toll of over 140,000 individuals. More than half of the brick buildings and one-tenth of the reinforced concrete structures in the region collapsed. Hundreds of thousands of homes were destroyed or burned in the ensuing fire touched off by the quake. The shock generated a tsunami that reached a height of 12m (39.5ft) at Atami, 97km south from Tokyo. The tsunami was so large that it that destroyed 155 houses and killed 60 people as far away as Sagami, approximately 32km from Tokyo. For the navy, the earthquake caused significant stress damage to *Amagi*'s hull and conversion work was abandoned; *Kaga* was ordered to replace her, but the *Akagi* did not suffer heavy damage, allowing conversion work to continue.

DESIGN

AKAGI AS AN AIRCRAFT CARRIER

On 19 November 1923, the decision was taken to convert *Akagi*, and over her completed armoured main deck, new hangars and the flight deck were built into the hull over it. Her four-shaft 132,000shp Giken turbine propulsion system was retained, but the conversion would reduce the overall ship's weight, and it was calculated that her speed would increase to 32.5 knots. With the change in weight and displacement, the draught of the original battlecruiser design and new aircraft carrier would be different, necessitating modification of the position and shape of the hull's side armour. The completed armour belt was removed and rerolled to a reduced thickness, and the shape of the forward end of the torpedo bulges was modified.

Model of *Akagi* as first converted to a carrier with members of the Kure naval arsenal design department. Pictured are Keiji Suzuki, Yuzuna Hiraga, Kakuji Suzuki, Kikoshi Nagamura, Kikuo Fujimoto, Shigeru Nakao, Tsunahiko Kubo, and Eikichi Yokota. *(Yamato Museum)*

Despite the experience gained with *Hōshō*, the conversion of a ship three times her size presented new and unexpected challenges, coupled with the rapidly developing world of naval aviation with heavier and faster aircraft. New flight deck characteristics had to be tested in a near trial-and-error fashion. The Japanese solution was inspired by Britain's *Furious* that had two flight decks to accommodate different types of aircraft, but the Japanese engineers determined that *Akagi* would require three. The top deck measured 190.2m long and ran the length of the ship, but stopped well short of the bow. This deck was for both take-off and landing, and carried no obstructions (*eg*, an island for command and navigation), but the aftermost section – about one-third – of the deck sloped downward towards the stern to present an incline to assist slowing and stopping landing aircraft. The second deck was called the *turret deck* and extended forward beyond the upper flight deck and was designed exclusively for the smallest and lightest aircraft. In theory this was a take-off deck only, with the ship's navigation bridge located at its rear in front of the hangars. However, during construction it was realized that the deck was too short (15m) for aircraft operations and it was blocked off and ceased to be a flight deck.

The ship's defensive armament comprised ten 20cm (7.9in) 3rd Year Type guns, in six single casemates aft and two twin Type B turrets sided forward on the

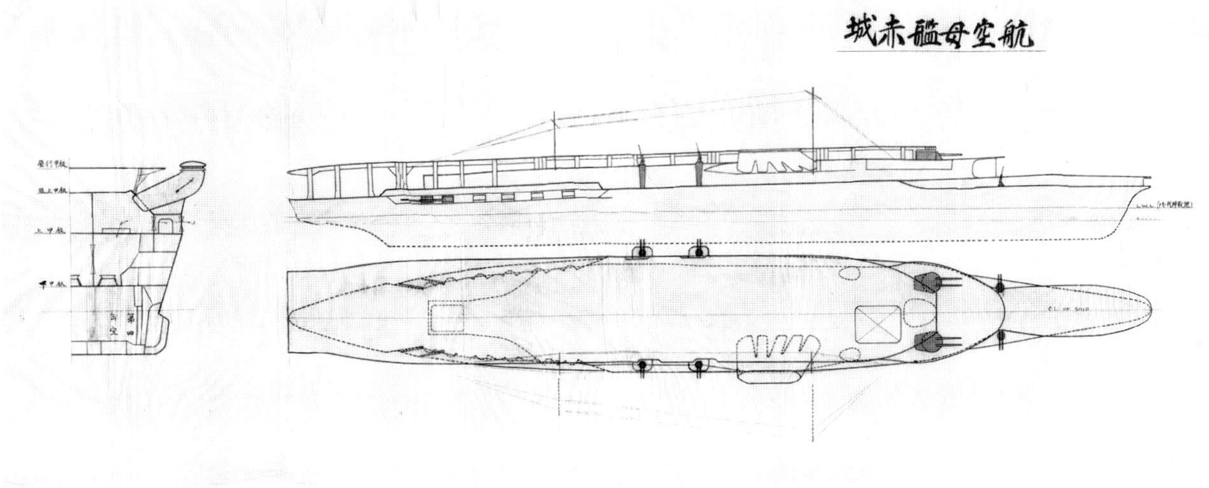

middle flight deck. They fired 110kg projectiles (three to six rounds per minute) with a muzzle velocity of 870m/s at 25° elevation for a maximum range between 22,600 and 24,000m. The Type B turrets were nominally capable of 70° elevation to provide additional anti-aircraft fire, but in practice the maximum elevation was only 55°, which coupled with their slow rate of fire and the fixed 5° loading angle minimized any useful anti-aircraft capability. These guns were primarily fitted as protection against encounters with enemy heavy cruisers which were thought to be the most significant threat to the ship, but it was also in keeping with the Decisive Battle Doctrine, the designers believing *Akagi* could potentially participate in a set piece battle. At this time, naval aviation was viewed as fleet *support* where aircraft were expected to provide reconnaissance, spotting, and interception of enemy aircraft. The Decisive Battle Doctrine dictated that major offensive attacks on an enemy vessel would be carried out by heavier land-based aircraft carrying large loads of torpedoes and bombs.

Studies of *Akagi*'s profile and plan view layouts as a carrier. These sketches were drawn on silk. *(University of Tokyo)*

A close-up view of *Akagi* under construction. Of note is the extensive lattice work and supports for the forward lower flight deck. *(University of Tokyo)*

The third and lowest deck at 56.7m long was for launching small aircraft. It may seem odd that such a short deck could be used for launching aircraft, but it must be remembered at the time of conversion, naval aircraft were light. The speed of the ship was near the stall speed of the aircraft and coupled with the aircraft's engine power, wind speed when turned into the wind, and rapid brake release on take-off that would catapult the aircraft forward to take off speed. The ship carried three hangars, one for each deck and an elevator fore and aft. The forward elevator was sized to handle large aircraft such as torpedo bombers. The aft elevator measured 12.8m x 8.4m to handle fighters and small reconnaissance aircraft.

The diversion of funnel gases away from the flight deck was a major problem. Experience from the *Hōshō* showed that smoke could be vented to the side of the ship, but the smoke often flowed upwards over the flight deck creating turbulence and hindering landing. Pilots also complained that a funnel or island on the deck obscured their vision during landing. The Japanese conducted extensive wind tunnel testing of funnel configurations at the Technical Research Institute (located at Lake Kasumigara, 60km NE of Tokyo). No clear solution was found, but by locating the main funnel amidships on the starboard side under the flight deck bent at 120° downwards and angled outwards, flanked by two smaller upward funnels, provided the best diversion of gases during landing operations. The funnel incorporated a series of vents into the rear of the upper side covered by removable plates. In an emergency, the plates could be removed, allowing the funnel gases to be released quickly upwards, supplemented by a seawater system that pumped water into any hot gas to cool it. The space requirement for the funnel trunking starboard amidships caused the upper flight deck to be raised on the port side, affecting the ship's centreline and subsequently the shape and location of anti-aircraft sponsons on each side.

Akagi was launched as an aircraft carrier on 22 April 1925 and completed on 25 March 1927. At completion, her length was 261.21m overall, with a beam of 31m and, at deep load, a draught of 8.08m. She displaced 27,300 tons at standard load, and 34,920 at full load. Her complement was 1600 and her air group consisted of 28 Mitsubishi B1M3 torpedo bombers, 16 Nakajima A1N fighters and 16 Mitsubishi 2MR reconnaissance aircraft.

KAGA AS AN AIRCRAFT CARRIER

Kaga's conversion commenced at Yokosuka Arsenal on 19 November 1923, and like *Akagi* had three flight decks and 20cm guns, but her hull was shorter, and she was slower. As a battleship her expected speed had been 26.5 knots, but the reduction in

Aircraft stowage on *Akagi*'s forecastle deck. *(Yamato Museum)*

displacement to 34,233 tons increased her speed to 27.5 knots. She had twelve Kampon Type B boilers, eight being oil-fired with the remainder burning an oil and coal mix. She carried 8128 tons of fuel oil and 1727 tons of coal to give her a range of 8000 nautical miles at 14 knots.

The principal difference between *Kaga* and *Akagi* was funnel placement. The Yokosuka naval constructors experimented with *Kaga*'s by initially fitting two large funnels, one on each side below the flight deck and close to the stern to force the gases aft. These were slanted diagonally and outward from the hull to vent the gases away from the ship. However, operational experience showed that this funnel placement impeded airflow at the stern and coupled with her lower speed did not force the funnel gases astern but instead sucked the funnel gases and smoke over the flight deck. Another consequence was that the living quarters for the warrant offers were located close to the funnel trunking which raised the cabin temperatures to an intolerable degree. The aft placement of the funnels also altered the centre of gravity of the ship, so they were moved amidships, saving in 1016 tons in weight with the removal of some trunking. However, this affected the ship's stability and addressing the issue delayed the completion of *Kaga*'s conversion until 31 March 1928, despite having been started before *Akagi*.

Kaga's flight deck also showed several differences from *Akagi* due to *Kaga's* hull being shorter and of greater beam. The upper flight deck extended for most of the length of *Kaga's* hull to obtain the required length to launch heavier aircraft, and the downward slope of the aft section was greater than *Akagi*'s to assist breaking and slowing these larger aircraft. On *Akagi* another reason her deck had less of a slope was because it was thought that in certain circumstances aircraft could land 'backwards' – coming in from the bow to stern. Too great a slope would allow the aircraft to pick up speed and increase the risk of rolling off the stern. The shape of the deck differed between the two ships when viewed from above. *Kaga's* aft deck was squared

Kaga under construction. *(Yamato Museum)*

An interesting view of *Kaga*'s wooden flight deck being laid. Molten tar caulking and oakum is applied between the deck planks much as in the age of sail. *(Yamato Museum)*

Port side forward view of *Kaga* completed as a three-decked carrier. *(Yamato Museum)*

The navigation bridge on *Kaga*'s middle flight deck. *(Yamato Museum)*

off, whereas *Akagi's* was bevelled, but the reason for the difference is not documented. The second and third flight decks were also wider than *Akagi*'s. The number and type of aircraft was to be the same as *Akagi*, but *Kaga*'s elevators were slightly larger with the forward one measuring 10.67m long x 15.85m wide and offset to starboard, and the aft measuring 12.8m long and 9.1m wide placed on the centreline, recognizing that the aircraft she would be carrying in future would be larger and heavier. The original arresting gear fitted was a vertical rope type (*ie*, cables were placed on raised stanchions on the deck and run through pulleys and attached to dead weights) that was changed to a horizontal rope type in both ships (*ie*, where the cables lie across the deck and fitted to rotary braking drums) manufactured by Schneider in France in 1931. These were replaced with domestically produced Kayaba brakes that used friction and hydraulic pressure. As originally completed, *Kaga* carried an air group of 28 Mitsubishi B1M3 torpedo bombers, 16 Nakajima A1N fighters and 16 Mitsubishi 2MR reconnaissance aircraft.

Kaga as completed had a length of 238.5m overall, a beam of 31.67m and a full load draught of 7.92m. She displaced 27,300 tons at standard load, and 34,234 tons at full load, nearly 6100 tons less than her designed displacement as a battleship. Her complement totalled 1340 crewmembers.

Shortly after *Kaga*'s conversion, her speed limitation, funnel arrangement problems, and the rapidly increasing size and weight of carrier torpedo and bombing aircraft made it clear that a second major reconstruction would be required. The impetus was a realization within the naval hierarchy of the changing role of naval aviation, which should now be able to launch major offensive operations against enemy capital ships within the Decisive Battle Doctrine. Land-based aircraft were no longer to be the primary means of paring down the enemy navy as it headed towards Japan. Aircraft carriers would now be formally classed as true capital ships in the Japanese Navy.

KAGA'S MODERNIZATION

The reconstruction was completed on 15 June 1934, with major changes that included the abolition of the three flight decks for single one that was as long as possible to handle the new aircraft. The deck was extended the full length of the hull with extensions fore and aft. The new deck measured 248.6m by 30.5m maximum breadth, and a third elevator was installed in the centre of the flight deck to serve the increased space created by extending the

Kaga at anchor off Yokohama in 1933. *(Yamato Museum)*

central hangar forward to house 72 aircraft with 18 in reserve.

A small island bridge structure was installed far forward on the starboard side and away from the aft deck to not obscure the landing pilot's vision. The funnels were incorporated into a single downward and diagonally bent exhaust on the starboard side midships that improved the venting of gases and coupled with the longer flight deck no longer obscured the aft flight deck. A single funnel also made it easier for the ship to be manoeuvred into favourable winds to blow the gases away from the ship during landing operations. Like *Akagi*, the funnel was fitted with a water-cooling system for the exhaust gases and a cover that could be raised to allow the gases to escape if the ship developed a severe list and the mouth of the funnel touched the sea. The space freed up by the removal of the funnel ducts was divided into two decks and converted into living quarters (now much more comfortable) for the expanded air group.

The height of the ship was lowered to help mitigate the inclining effect of wind pressure on the hull sides, but the weight savings and redistribution again shifted the vessel's centre of gravity. To compensate for the ship's tendency to roll and risk of capsizing (as measured by *metacentric height* or the initial static stability of a floating body), her hull was lengthened by 10.3m at the stern, which also reduced drag, and her waterline armoured belt was reduced from 280mm to 152mm. Additional armour was added to the torpedo bulges and to her underwater hull above the side armour abreast the upper part of the existing bulge to increase her beam, that also contributed to lowering her centre of gravity and increasing stability. Her deck armour was also reduced from 102mm to 38mm.

It has been suggested by some writers that the design of the aviation fuel storage tanks posed an unrealized danger to the ship. Aviation fuel was carried in two groups of tanks, one forward and the other abaft the machinery spaces. Each group of tanks was divided into two sections, one

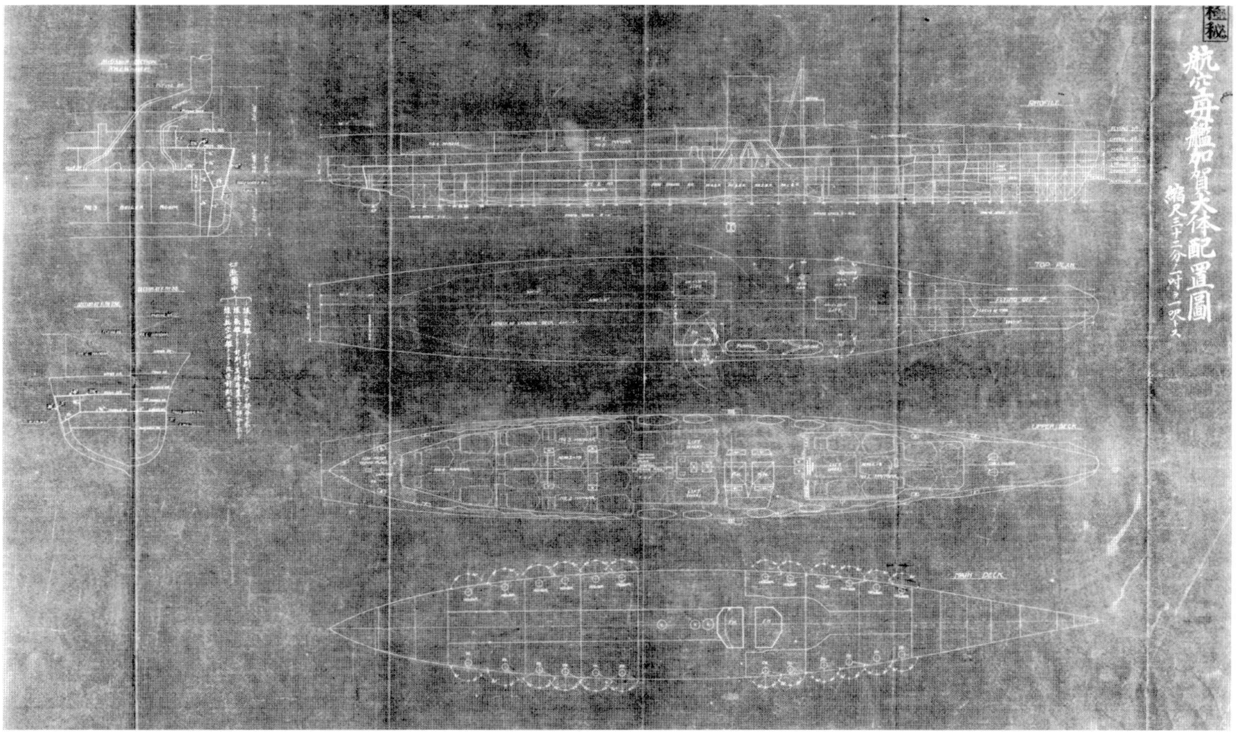

section containing high octane fuel (for starting up aircraft and providing high bursts or speed), the other containing a lower octane fuel used by aircraft for cruising. The danger arose where the aviation fuel tanks formed part of the ship's structure, that is where a hull bulkhead, or deck formed part of the storage tank. These tanks were double skinned to surround the fuel compartment with an air space filled with inert carbon dioxide gas (CO_2) to reduce the chances of explosive vapour forming. The aviation gasoline pumping machinery space was situated either just above or alongside the tanks and contained three separate pumps: one for high octane fuel, one for low octane fuel, and the third for dirty water and bilge water such as water from sinks and showers, but not toilets. In an emergency, the space above the aviation gasoline in the tanks, pump spaces, valve and working compartments, could be filled with CO_2. However, the integrity of the fuel tank was dependent upon the ship's ability to absorb the shock of a bomb, mine, shell, torpedo or depth-charge. Any shock was transferred directly to the tank increasing the risk of cracks and ruptures forming. The weakness of the system was realized in later carrier designs such as the *Taiho* where the top and side air spaces were filled with concrete as a further protection against bomb damage.

However, Japanese drawings suggest otherwise. The plans showing the aviation fuel system suggest that most of the fuel tanks were not part of the structure of the ship, but were *self-contained* vessels akin to British designs. British aviation fuel was stored in tanks standing free of the ship's structure and situated in armoured areas of the hull. British designs were superior in that the interiors of the aviation storage tanks were compartmentalized with coffer-dams so that the fuel was surrounded by seawater. In this way, a shock to the ship would not be directly transmitted to the fuel tanks, and if a fuel tank was ruptured, the fuel would spill into an environment already filled with liquid – significantly reducing the chance of fire or dangerous vapour concentrations. This method meant that less fuel could be carried but the reduction in fire risk was a valuable trade-off in action.

Perhaps the most significant design flaw was that the aircraft hangars were fully

A plan of the proposed modernization of *Kaga* about 1925. *(University of Tokyo)*

Schematic of Japanese aviation fuel storage tank and pumping. The drawing shows a stand-alone tank quite separate from the hull sides, floor, and ceiling of the ship's structure. *(University of Tokyo)*

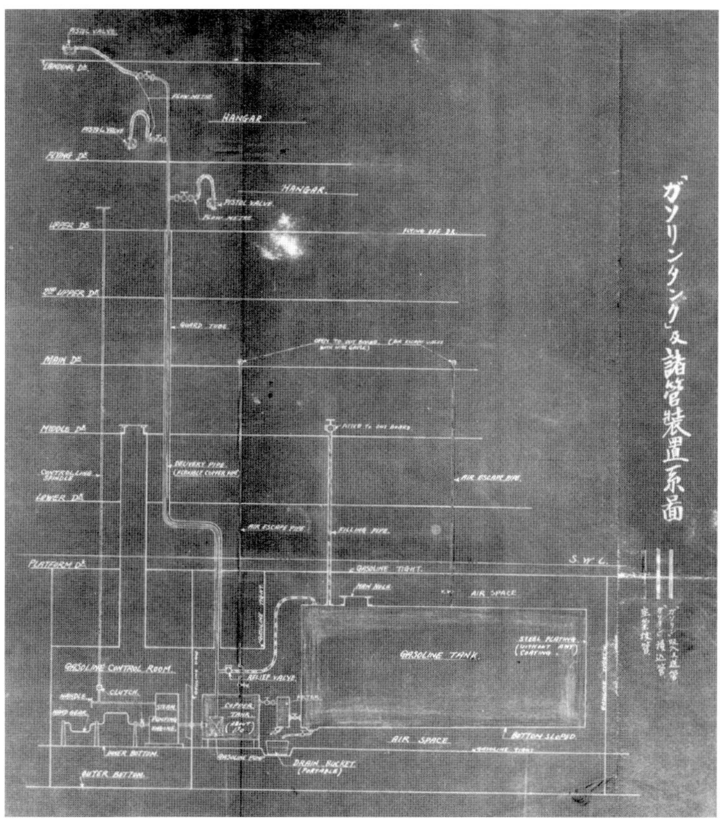

Kaga's aft flight deck under construction during her modernization. *(Yamato Museum)*

enclosed structures and the extensive number of refuelling points within the hangar led inevitably to spills and vapour forming. The hangar's aircraft filling positions were supplied by two main fuel lines, one for the A type (high octane) fuel and the other for lower octane B type fuel. These mains were situated in the middle section of the lower hangar and in the end sections of the upper hangar. On the upper hangar these filling points were in the middle section of the hangar and up to the flight deck. Sufficient fixed Type A filling positions were provided to ensure that any position, in either hangars or flight deck, could be reached with a 25-metre flexible metal hose. Twice as many filling positions were provided for Type B fuel. Planes were defuelled by hose into hoppers at convenient points in the hangar. Any spilled fuel and how the fuel and vapours were discharged posed a fire and explosion hazard.

During emergency situations each hangar was divided into sections by closing a fireproof roller door, relying on a system of fresh air intake and exhaust fans to ventilate the closed off sections. The intake fan arrangements brought fresh air onto one side of the hangar at a height of four to five feet above the deck and with exhaust fans placed on the sides at just above deck level. Fan capacities were based on a complete renewal of the air in the hangar in 10 minutes. However, because funnel gases passed downwards through curved funnels on the starboard side, all the supply intakes were on the port side, and the exhausts ports on the starboard side were often closed to avoid drawing funnel gases into the hangar. As a result, with the ports closed the exhaust fans had an unnoticed tendency to set up a circulation of air in the hangar along the ship's longitudinal axis and produced an undesirable and dangerous mechanical mixing of air and fuel vapours that counteracted the natural tendency of fuel vapours to form a blanket on the bottom of the hangar that could be expelled off the ship as designed. Moreover, wherever possible the location of the fan compartments was placed outside hangar bulkheads but because the location of the funnel uptakes, boiler room down-takes, and passageways sometimes necessitated placing them *inside* the hangar which helped concentrate fumes within the enclosed space.

The danger from vapours was increased because operational doctrine dictated that aircraft be serviced, fuelled, and armed in the hangars whenever possible to keep the deck open for flying operations, whereas American doctrine used the hangars for storage and repair, with refuelling and rearming carried out on deck to increase efficiency by not having to bring the aircraft below. Japanese ships also did not have any redundancy in the fire-extinguishing system, so any damage to this vital network was terminal. The enclosed hangars were also problematic in battle situations. In the case of a bomb hit, the force of the explosion was contained by the hangar sides, unlike in American carriers where explosions could be vented through the sides and vertically, greatly reducing the effects of the blast.

The reconstruction removed the two twin 20cm gun turrets but retained the six 20cm guns in the aft hull casemates and increased them to ten. *Kaga*'s anti-aircraft armament was improved to comprise eight 12cm 10th Year Type Model A2 twin gun mounts fitted on sponsons at the level of the funnel but that reduced their effectiveness by hampering any fire across the flight deck. These guns fired 20.3kg projectiles at a muzzle velocity of 825–830m/s at 45° with a maximum range of 16,000m. The guns had a maximum ceiling 10,000m at 75° elevation. Their effective rate of fire was six to eight rounds per minute. The ship had two Type 89 directors to control her 20cm guns and two Type 91 manually powered anti-aircraft directors to control her 12cm guns. A battery of 11 twin mounted 25mm guns completed her anti-aircraft armament. They fired 0.25-kg projectiles at a muzzle velocity of 900m/s at 50° elevation to a maximum range of 7500m and of 5500 m ceiling. The effective rate of fire was only between 110 and 120 rounds per minute due to the frequent need to change the 15-round magazines.

Half of the ship's turbines (Brown-Curtis type) were replaced with two Japanese designed Kanemoto type and her boilers were Kampon Type B with a working pressure of $22kg/cm^2$ (2157 kPa) at a temperature of 300°C. Power output increased from 90,000 to 125,000shp and the ship could now make 28.3 knots, up from the previous 27.5 knots. Her fuel storage was increased to 7620 tons of fuel oil which increased her endurance to 10,000nm (19,000km) at 16 knots. The ship also received new propellers.

The arresting gear was replaced with the Kure Type 4 system that had a braking capacity of four tons. The Kure type used electromagnets. The two ends of a wire were led to the two sides of a winding drum inside and affixed to a squirrel cage made of high resistance bronze. The drum and cage rotated around a six-pole stator energized with 120 amperes at 220 volts at the maximum. To reset the wire the current in the stator was reversed. With the help of a supporting mechanism the wire was stretched across the deck at a prescribed height. When the landing plane caught the wire, the drum rotated and generated electric energy that was used to stop the plane. The Type 4 could stop a four-ton aircraft travelling at a speed of 30mps (acceleration 2.0Gs) in less than 40 metres. The released wire could be retrieved in twelve seconds. Eight arresting wires were fitted to her flight deck. The carrier's complement increased to 1708 crew-members.

AKAGI'S MODERNIZATION

Reconstruction work began on 24 October 1935 at Sasebo Naval Yard and was completed on 31 August 1938. Her modernization largely mirrored *Kaga*'s, with the General Naval Staff requirements specifying: 1) a single flight deck that was long enough to provide sufficient runway for the new naval attack aircraft; 2) a small island on the flight deck to better manage ship and aircraft operations; 3) the hangar enlarged to carry more aircraft; 4) greater anti-aircraft protection, and increased space to carry aircraft fuel, bombs and torpedoes – sufficient for sustained operations of three waves of attack; 5) the ship's boilers reconfigured to only use heavy fuel oil instead of distillates because of its low

Starboard forward view of *Akagi* underway in 1938. *(Yamato Museum)*

Port side forward view of *Akagi*. *(Yamato Museum)*

cost, and; 6) the funnels reshaped to curve further downward.

In compliance, *Akagi's* two funnels were incorporated into a single casing that was wider and thicker than *Kaga*'s and retained the emergency seawater system and removable casing plates to cool funnel gases in an emergency. The single flight deck measured 249.2m long by 30.5m wide and inclined down slightly fore and aft from a point about three-eighths of the way aft to assist aircraft taking off and landing, respectively. A total of eight expansion joints were fitted to the flight deck to prevent buckling due to wave-generated hull flexing. Both *Akagi* and *Kaga* were fitted with an aircraft-shielding wind-break installed in front of the forward elevator. It was not solid but approximately 30 per cent of its surface was covered with perforations. The screen was designed to withstand up to 50mps deck wind and could be raised against a 35mps wind in less than 30 seconds. To assist in securing aircraft, the deck area was studded with flush mounted tie-down eyebolts.

Unlike *Kaga*, the island was located on the port side at the centre of the flight deck. The reason for this was the conclusion that *Kaga*'s bridge was too far forward, obstructing the view of pilots taking off at the cost of improving the field of view of the deck during landing. Several experiments showed that the best location was near the centre of the flight deck, and the bridge was situated on the port side to be opposite the funnel on the starboard side whose gases could therefore not blow directly into the bridge. The eleven main coal/oil-fired boilers were replaced with nineteen modern Japanese Ku-go boilers that could burn the heavy fuel oil. Although engine output increased from 131,200 to 133,000shp, her speed declined slightly from 32.5 to 31.2 knots on trials because of the increase in her displacement to 46,255 tons. Her bunkerage was increased to 7620 tons of fuel oil which increased her endurance to 10,000nm at 16 knots. Like the *Kaga*, the two forward 20cm gun turrets were removed but the six casemate guns retained and controlled by a single Type 89 director. Anti-aircraft armament was increased to six 12cm twin anti-aircraft guns and fourteen twin 25mm guns. However, the ship's anti-aircraft guns were grouped amidships and placed low on the hull so could not be brought to bear directly forward or aft. The placement of the island also blocked the forward arcs of the port battery.

Both *Akagi* and *Kaga* had three hangar decks. On *Akagi* her fore elevator could only access the upper and middle hangars, but the rear elevator was able to service all three hangar decks. On the *Kaga*, her elevators could only access the top and middle hangars, with her lower hangar accessed by a service elevator between the lower and middle hangar decks. Aircraft from the lower deck had to be moved to the middle hangar before moving through the upper hangar to the flight deck. These arrangements caused delays in aircraft handing that could hinder flight operations.

Many of the design issues of both ships noted here were the product of converting a battleship to a carrier at a time when naval aviation, doctrine, and experience was in its infancy. Trial and error were very much the order of the day, and the innovation, industry and persistence of the Japanese designers and builders was remarkable.

Model Products

Both *Akagi* and *Kaga* are extremely popular subjects in Japan, and the sheer number of new kits, special edition reissues, and accessory sets ensures that a kit of one or both ships is available in virtually any model shop at any time. What follows is a round-up of recently available kits that only scratches the surface of what is available.

FUJIMI FIRST AIR FLEET ***AKAGI*** AND ***KAGA***
(KIT #401362) 1:3000 scale

Fujimi has released a series of diminutive 1:3000 scale models of virtually every Imperial Navy ship. The kits are sold in sets that commemorate specific events (*eg*, Midway Sea Operation, Hawaii Operation) or naval bases such as Kure complete with diorama bases with buildings and a clear blue seascape or sets of just the ships themselves. The set to hand contains models of *Akagi*, *Kaga* and the *Fubuki* class destroyers *Akebono*, *Ushio*, *Sazanami*, and *Oboro*. In this scale the hull of *Akagi* measures just 85mm, *Kaga*, 83mm, and the destroyers 38mm long. Despite their small size, the models are highly detailed and the moulding crisp and devoid of any chunky overscale details. The carriers are assembled from three parts, whereas the destroyers are single castings. Items like gun barrels are moulded solid with the deck or hull but are very fine and well-defined making painting easy. Ship's boats on the quarterdeck are also well defined with almost scale like detail. Perhaps the only obvious oversimplification are the masts

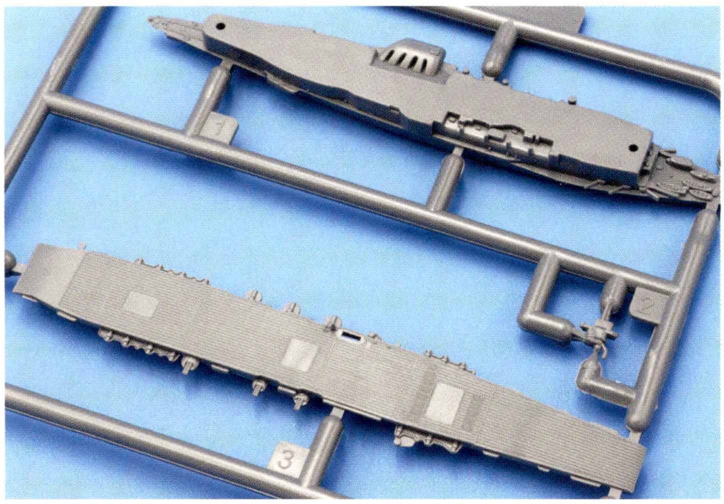

A remarkable amount of crisp detail has been moulded into the main carrier castings.

which are moulded solid, but for those with the eyesight and manual dexterity, they can be cut away and replaced with etched brass items that Fujimi offer for the range of ships. A set of decals are provided for the flight deck markings, but no aircraft are included. Fujimi opted not to mould aircraft to the flight deck but left the decks clear as if all aircraft are below. For those wanting aircraft, several free 3D printing files (*.stl* files) available for the Vals, Zeros, and Kates that can be scaled down to 1:3000 and printed by oneself. In all, these tiny models are suitable for wargamers, but a boon to diorama builders for their scale and jewel-like qualities allowing the ships to be portrayed at much more realistic distances from one another.

FUJIMI ***AMAGI*** (KIT #401041) AND ***AKAGI*** (KIT #401164) BATTLECRUISERS
1:700 scale

No collection of Japanese aircraft carriers would be complete without these two 'what if' battlecruiser kits. The crisply moulded kit parts are identical in both kits, depicting the ships as they would have appeared if completed as battle-cruisers. Minute detail is featured such as deck planks rendered as fine recessed lines, refined starfish and mast parts, and the casemate guns detailed with realistic blast bags with delicate barrels. Searchlights are moulded in clear plastic, and the aircraft

During their construction as battlecruisers their design was continuously under review and there were plans to replace the two upright funnels with a single trunked one. This funnel design is shown in the background ship rendering (presumably *Amagi*) seen on the *Akagi*'s kit box art.

the ship was to carry include miniscule moulded interplane struts. Building and displaying *Akagi* as a battlecruiser, a three-decked carrier, and as a single-deck carrier would make for an interesting display showing the evolution of the ship. For *Kaga*, no conventional plastic kits of a *Tosa* class battleship exist to make a similar display.

HASEGAWA *KAGA* (KIT #202) AND *KAGA* 'SUPER DETAIL' (KIT #30015) 1:700 scale

The original tooling for the kit was first released in 1973, and in 1992 (Kit #202) was revised to include sets of nicely detailed generic ship's boats, guns and other small fittings to replace the simplified kit parts. The generic fret of parts are the same as supplied in many Aoshima and Fujimi kits as well. The original ship mouldings remain crisp, and a dry fit of the parts show they go together well. The age of the kit is exposed by the fact that the flight deck planking is rendered by fine *raised* moulded lines, and that all the flight deck markings are moulded onto the deck. No decals are provided for the deck markings, and these will have to be painted by the modeller. It would also be hard to remove these moulded markings because any sanding will also damage the fine planking detail. Hasegawa suggest the deck is painted tan for the wooden sections and grey for the metal portions with the deck markings lightly dry brushed with white paint to define their outlines that are filled in using a fine brush. It would be much simpler to paint the deck white, mask off the markings with strips of tape and paint the rest of the deck tan and grey. The airwing is a single sprue of eight A6M2s (Allied code name 'Zero'), four Type 99 dive bombers (Allied code name 'Val'), and four B5N bombers (Allied code name 'Kate'). Generic aircraft markings are provided consisting of little more than red sun disc markings or *hinomaru* for the fuselage and wings.

Out-of-the-box, the kit will build into a nice if somewhat simplified model of *Kaga*, but it provides the modeller an excellent base to build a detailed model using scratch-built parts and taking advantage of the plethora of aftermarket parts (*eg*, like replacement guns, boats, Carley floats, hatches and doors, wooden decks and etch sets). The range of 1:700 scale accessories for Japanese ships is enormous and what is not designed specifically for this kit of *Kaga* can be readily adapted from other sets.

The 'Super Detail' version of the kit was released in 1991 with a fret of etched steel details like open lattice work girders, railings sized for specific sections of the ship, flight deck netting, aircraft propellers, and funnel grille. This version of the kit does not include the new generic frets of ship's fittings.

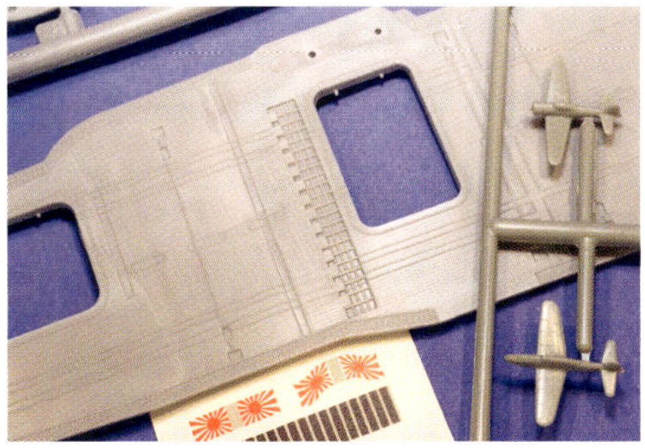

The raised detail of planking and tread plate – and deck markings moulded on the flight deck.

FUJIMI 'NEXT' *AKAGI* (KIT #460512) 1:700 scale

The NEXT line of kits is an innovative range of pre-coloured press-fit kits that deliver a highly detailed and accurate model with virtually no painting. They are designed much like the hugely popular kits based on the *Gundam* anime series that features giant robots (or *mecha*) in a futuristic militaristic setting that are moulded in several colours on each part sprues. The NEXT ship range has become incredibly popular and Fujimi has released kits of all the major Imperial Navy vessels. The kits can also be built like conventional kits with glue and painted, and all kits are full hull. Their *Akagi* features a multitude of sprues moulded in grey for the hull superstructure, tan for the deck, red for the lower hull and rudder, gold for the screws, red brown for the linoleum quarterdeck, off-white for the Zero and Val aircraft, and deep green for the Kates. The parts are crisply moulded and feature high-definition details. Most notable are the supports that hold up the flight deck, some of the lattice work being moulded as open. A host of tiny details including binoculars are provided, and refined AA and casemate guns are provided. The aircraft are detailed with delicate recessed panel lines, but also with convincing airscrews moulded directly to the engine cowlings. The landing gear is provided as separate parts, complete with spats for the Vals. A black moulded display stand for the ship is included. Test fitting of major parts shows a precise fit and the design of the kit ensures that the join

The multicoloured sprues of the kit obviates painting.

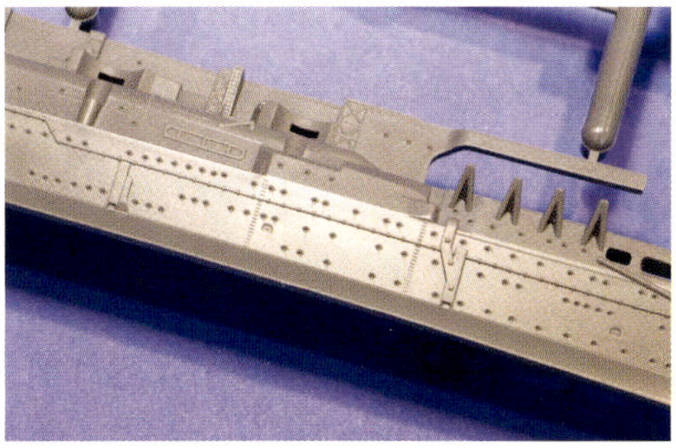
The superb detail characteristic of the press-fit 'Next' kit range.

between parts fall on major lines to hide their presence. A good pair of nippers will be necessary to remove moulding pips which are often moulded on the joint face, not the part side to preserve detail and the neatness of the join. Once the parts are press-fit, they will be hard to take apart such is the precision of the tolerances, so beware.

Finishing the kit will take some thought. If opting for the pre-coloured method, no doubt there will be some sanding marks and flaws that are normally hidden by a coat of paint. To remove these flaws, one could polish the plastic to match the sheen of the other parts, or after assembly give the model a coat of semi-matt or matt varnish. Stickers are provided for the flight deck and linoleum decks. Notably, the linoleum deck stickers are printed with metallic inks to represent the brass strips that held the linoleum plates together. Stickers are also provided to decorate the ship's boats with white canvas covers or tan coloured printed thwarts and floors for the open boats. The aircraft *hinomarus* are well printed stickers. A waterslide decal is provided for the main flight deck for those opting for building and painting the model in the conventional way.

A very detailed model is readily produced from this well designed and engineered kit. It caters to the hobbyist looking for a simplified way of getting a model ship, or to one new to ship models – but it does not neglect the enthusiast who appreciates fine detail and fit to which one's own skills can be brought to get even more out of the kit.

HASEGAWA ***AKAGI*** (KIT #227) 1:700 scale

This kit was released in 2014 replacing their 1995 offering. Out-of-the-box the kit builds into a fine representation of the ship. Typical of this manufacturer, the parts breakdown and count make for easy and swift assembly. Moulded hull details like scuttles, and support girders are finely rendered. The flight deck planking is represented by recessed lines and not overdone, as is the underdeck girder detail yielding a realistic representation in this scale. The forecastle deck is ably detailed with scale anchor chain and distinct, but not obtrusive chequer-plate detail. The same chequer-plate detail is found on the quarterdeck and AA gun sponsons that look just right. Her distinctive funnel is detailed with raised foot rails and plate detail. Casemate and AA guns are also very delicate, and a few parts like side cranes are moulded as open lattices. The flightdeck supports are solid pieces but recesses representing lightening holes or lattice detail are deep, an effect that could be further heightened with black or very dark grey paint. A notable omission from the kit – and virtually all kits of the *Akagi* (and *Kaga*) – are the rolled splinter matting that covered the bridge sides. These can be made from rolled two-part epoxy putty, or from aftermarket accessory kits that sometimes include these items.

The airwing is represented by a single sprue containing eight Zeroes (three are not

used), four Vals, and four Kates. A large decal sheet provides all the flight deck markings and optional markings for the Pearl Harbor Operation (1941) or Midway Sea Operation in 1942. The aircraft mouldings are simplified with a little panel line detail, the landing gear represented by simple pegs, and an airscrew spinner but no propeller. The decal sheet shines in that extensive markings for the aircraft are provided. Besides the *hinomarus*, coloured fuselage and tail bands, tail code numbers, horizontal tailplane drift markings, and wing walk markings for specific named aircraft are provided to create an accurate and realistic airwing to place on the deck. The aircraft painting instructions are quite detailed. The decal sheet finishes off with several naval ensigns and admiral flags. One flag prints the Admiral's flag above of the battle ensign because the ensign was flown from the central gaff whereas the Admiral's flag was flown from a gaff to the side. This kit has been the subject of several aftermarket details sets offering a self-adhesive wood veneer flight deck, etched brass for the flight deck supports and structures, railings, and highly detailed 3D printed parts for the ship's boats, funnel, bridge, and even mainmast, among many other items. The fine detail of this kit coupled with excellent fit of parts and reasonable price has made this kit a firm favourite among modellers in Japan and abroad.

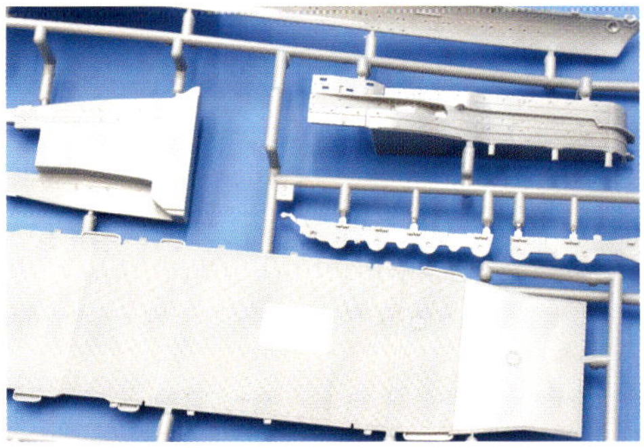

Fine detail and recessed deck planking is a feature of this kit.

HASEGAWA *AKAGI* 'PEARL HARBOR ATTACK'
(KIT #SP474) 1:700 scale

This 2020 limited edition kit, instructions, and decal sheet is identical to *Akagi* kit #227. What the special edition adds to this reissue by Hasegawa is a paper insert describing the composition of the First Air Fleet that attacked Pearl Harbor and a drawing of the fleet's track there and back. No information contained in the potted history is new. The other item is an embroidered patch emblazoned with the katakana characters トラ! トラ! トラ! (Tora Tora Tora), the codeword for the successful attack on Pearl Harbor – the abbreviation for 'lightning attack'.

HASEGAWA *AKAGI* FULL HULL VERSION 'BATTLE OF MIDWAY' (KIT #CH127) 1:700 scale

This special edition release from 2024 provides the same kit, instructions, and decals as *Akagi* (Kit #227). However, this release provides the parts to build a full hull version of the ship. Two new sprues moulded in red provide the additional underwater hull, bilge keels, and shafts. An unfinished wooden plinth is provided as a base to display the model that can be stained or oiled as desired. The final new parts are in soft white metal, including a set of screws, and – as a first – two sets of rolled

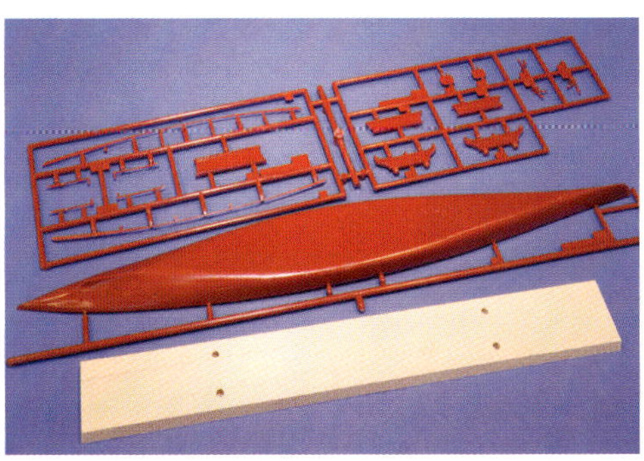

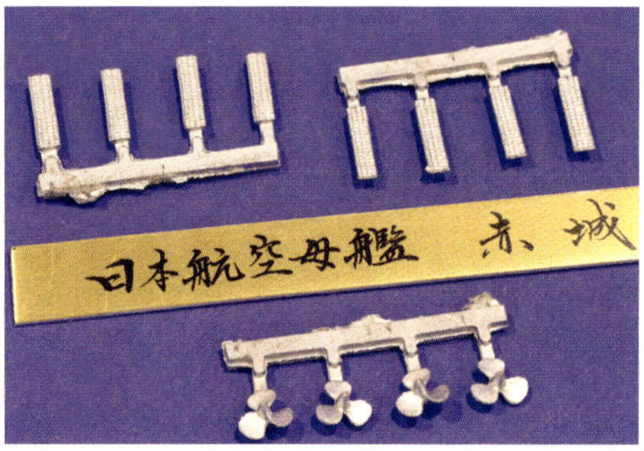

The white metal castings are rough and pitted.

splinter paddings. The metal parts are neatly cast but display some surface pitting, probably caused by the white metal cooling too quickly in the mould, that will have to be polished out. The splinter padding is cast as a straight row and must be bent to fit around the bridge structure with your fingers (using metal pliers will damage the surface of the soft metal). A nice variation of the basic kit and the wooden plinth make for a classy display model.

FUJIMI *AKAGI* (KIT #433615) AND *AKAGI* FULL HULL (KIT #451303) 1:700 scale

These two kits are the most detailed and in-scale of all the 1:700 *Akagi* kits. Kit #433615 was released in 2019 as a waterline kit and re-released as a full hull version in 2025. The detail moulded into the hull is what can be best described as the most complete. For example, the scuttles have extremely fine rigols, unlike the usual kit representations (whenever they are included) as over-thick brows. The foot ropes on the funnel are also very fine and not the usual heavy raised lines; and the flight deck planking is so delicate they are hard to discern, as they should appear in 1:700 scale. The underdeck support structures are daintily moulded, and although the support pillars are moulded solid, they feature realistic and prominent lattice work detail. The tread plate around the ship is also finely rendered. The attention to detail

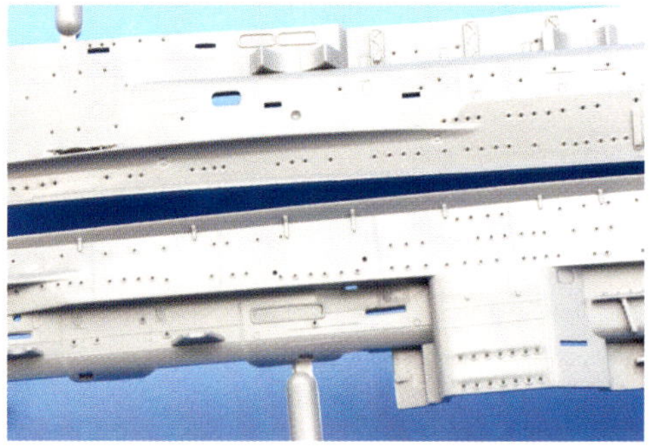

is remarkable: for example, the ship's boat davits have reinforcing rib detail, and the rope falls include tiny block and tackle details. The aircraft are extremely well detailed, with landing gear, airscrew, bombs and belly tanks provided as individual detailed parts. The box lid says in Japanese that the anti-aircraft armaments are made up from two pieces with separate pieces for barrels and mountings in order to include detail not possible if the item was moulded in one piece. The twin and triple AA guns are moulded so fine that they have reached the limits of injection moulding technology, and these are attached to mounts that are half the size of the same items found in other kits. The sprues also provide single AA mounts where each miniscule gun is fixed to a tiny base. The use of a magnifier is needed to appreciate the detail worked into the parts. The kit provides several generic sprues that hold scale hatches and ready-use boxes. Although these parts are not called out on the instructions, they are provided to the modeller to use as they please using photos of the ship for their locations near the AA guns. The searchlights are highly detailed and thoughtfully moulded in clear plastic to best represent their lenses. Despite all the included detail, the bridge is not provided with the splinter padding so prominent on the ship.

A decal sheet provides all the markings appropriate for 1941, and generic *hinomarus* for the airwing. Fuselage and tail markings will have to be hand painted or taken from another source, such as the Hasegawa Kit #227 of *Akagi*. For the full

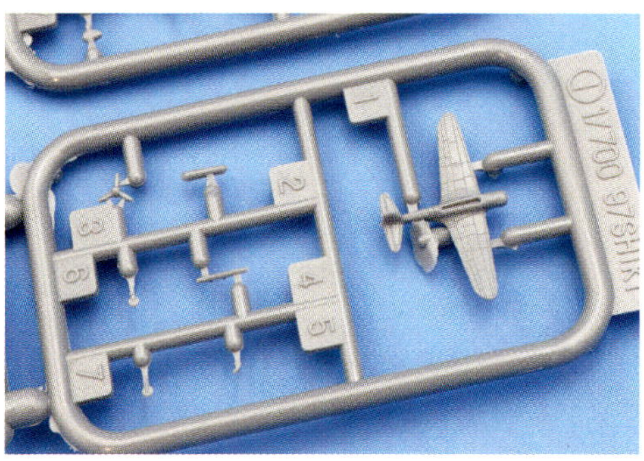

Each aircraft of the airwing is composed of several individual parts topped off with a separate clear canopy (not shown).

hull version, the underwater hull option provides a lower hull in red plastic along with shafts and screws, and the bilge keel is moulded into the hull and not separate parts like their NEXT version kit. A black plastic display stand rounds out the package. Out-of-the-box the kit will assemble into the most detailed model of *Akagi* and requires the least in the way of aftermarket accessories. After examination of the kit details, if the modeller wants to add etched railings, ensure that they are fine enough to match the fineness of the kit parts. Regular 1:700 railing is often over-scale, and this kit makes a case for not bothering to add it at all.

HASEGAWA *AKAGI* 'THREE FLIGHT DECK' (KIT #220) AND OPTIONAL HASEGAWA WOODEN DECK (ITEM #72124)

1:700 scale

Akagi's emergence as an aircraft carrier is neatly portrayed by this well moulded and engineered kit. Typical of Hasegawa, the detail is petite and understated. The part count is surprisingly low for such a complicated ship and guarantees a straightforward and pleasurable build. All three decks are well detailed with recessed deck planks, and the realistically portrayed underdeck system of girders and supports. The airwing consists of six Carrier Attack Bomber Type 13 Model 2 and six Carrier Fighter Type 90 biplanes. The aircraft carry wing rib detail and fully opened cockpit stations. The upper wing has a very tiny stub to represent the cabane struts that attaches to the top of the fuselage. The landing gear is a separate part and for the Type 13 Attack Bomber the torpedo is also a tiny, detailed part complete with props and screw boss. The first of the kit's decal sheet provides flight deck markings, naval ensigns, and nameplate in *kanji* (is a form of the Japanese writing taken from the Chinese characters). The second sheet is extensive containing *hinomarus*, rudder and fuselage tail codes and bands, and upper and lower wing codes for the airwing.

The centrepiece of the optional detail set are the self-adhesive wooden deck overlays.

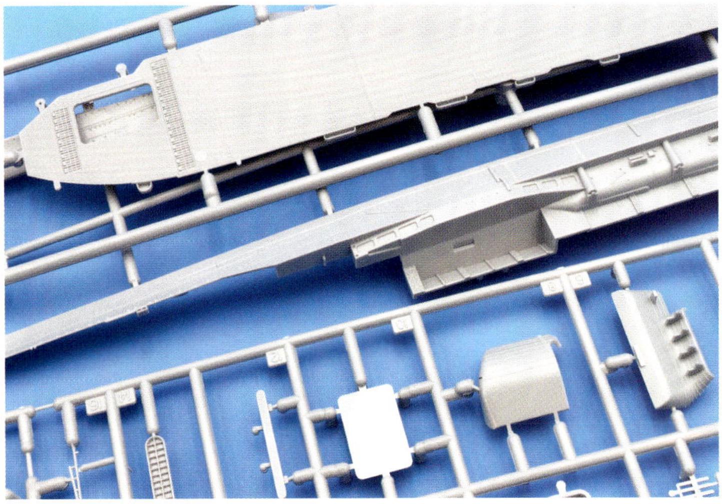

Often, wooden deck overlays, despite being made of wood, paradoxically, do not look like wood. This is because the wood veneer is often overprinted by inks with planking details to hide some obvious grain in the sheet or are too thick and it looks like an *ad hoc* addition that sticks out like a sore thumb. Not so with this Hasegawa accessory. The overlays are laser-cut and detailed from a very thin wood veneer that has no noticeable grain. The deck planking detail is about as close as one can get to

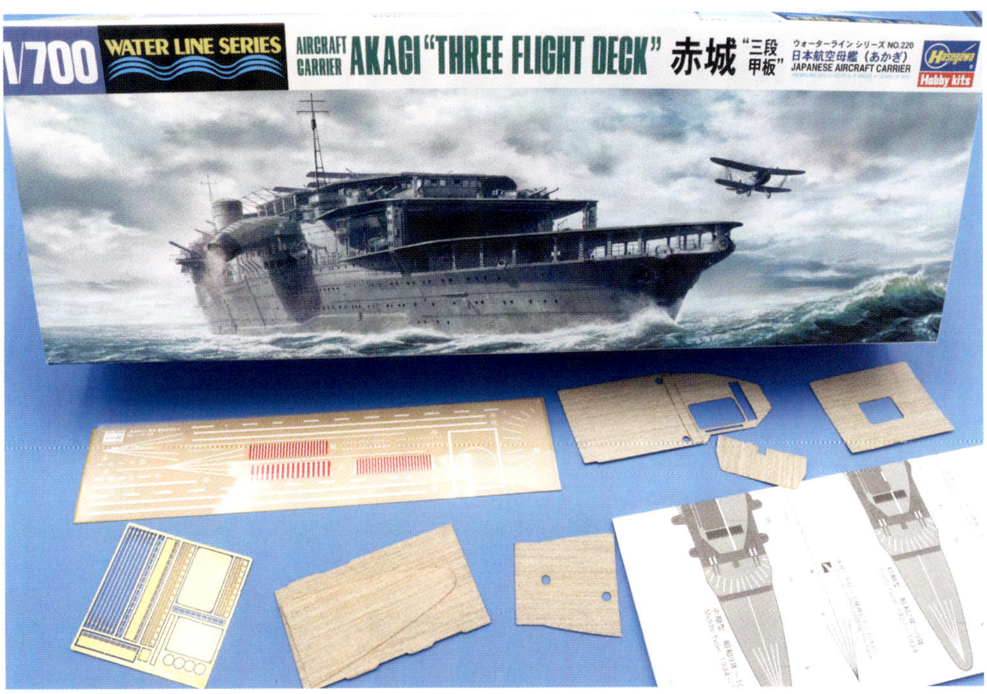

The optional wooden deck set brings a nice period feel to this early carrier.

1:700, and the laser etching is light and realistic. Applying waterslide decals to the wood veneer would certainly cause them to swell and buckle. To overcome this,

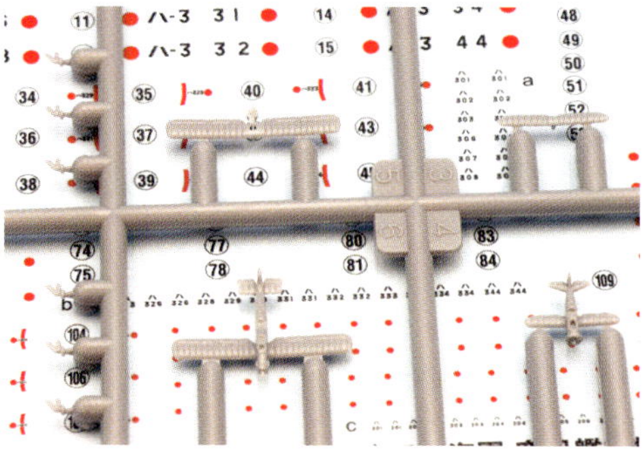

The diminutive biplanes are assembled from several tiny parts. The rib detail is a little heavy but after painting does not detract from the final result. The decal sheet for the aircraft is extensive, with multiple markings for each aircraft.

Hasegawa provides rub down dry transfers for the deck markings. One must take care with rub down transfers as rubbing too hard may leave dents in the wooden deck, or they may not release at all. An alternative is to have a custom paint mask made to spray on the deck markings with paint. One company that makes custom masks is *Kit Masx* from Canada. A small etched brass set is included to restore all the moulded flight deck detail covered up by the wooden overlay. This fret includes parts for arresting wires, crash barriers, deck hatches and elevators. This wooden deck set will enhance the basic model, but like most speciality parts, costs as much, if not a little more, than the base kit itself.

FUJIMI *KAGA* 'THREE TIER FLIGHT DECK' FULL HULL (KIT #451558) 1:700 scale

This is a superb kit of *Kaga*'s first incarnation as an aircraft carrier. The attention to detail and finesse is no different from this company's kits of *Akagi* (#433615

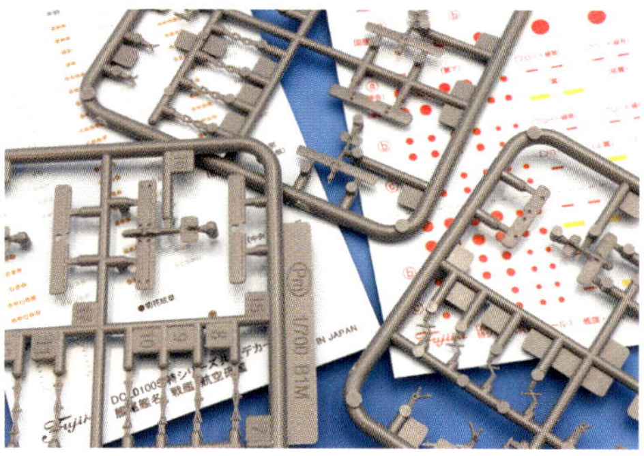

The biplanes are neatly moulded but the interplane struts and rigging will not do. Full marks to Fujimi for trying.

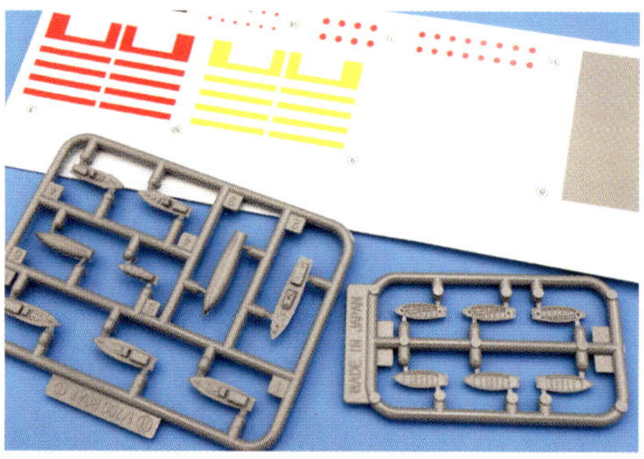

The ship's boats feature fine detail and, in a first, moulded oar detail on the boats' thwarts. The extensive decal sheet prints some colours separately to avoid registration issues.

& #451303) and the same comments apply. The details are moulded as in-scale as possible, and some supports and lattices are moulded open. A nice touch is that the ship's open boats have moulded oars sitting on top of the thwarts. The ship's infamous funnels are provided as separate parts to fix to the hull and here one gets a very clear impression of how large and long these trunkings were – and how hot and uncomfortable the cabins all along the length of the ship must have been. The flight decks are neatly detailed with deck planking or delicate representations of chequer plate. A large decal sheet gives the deck markings, and interestingly all the colours are printed separately. In this way, there are no registration problems and any misregistration is the modeller's fault.

The airwing includes two of Type 10 C1M reconnaissance planes, Type 13 BM1 torpedo attack planes, and Type 3 A1N2 fighters. The aircraft carry exquisite detail and strutted and spatted landing gear and torpedoes are separate parts. The aircraft are also provided with separate interplane struts complete with rigging. Sadly, these are far too heavy for scale. The holes for the struts are moulded into the top of the lower wing and bottom of the top wing so the fastidious modeller can fit tiny lengths of brass rod or stretched sprue into the holes. Two sheets of decals provide *hinomarus* as well as accurate tail codes and fuselage stripes for the aircraft.

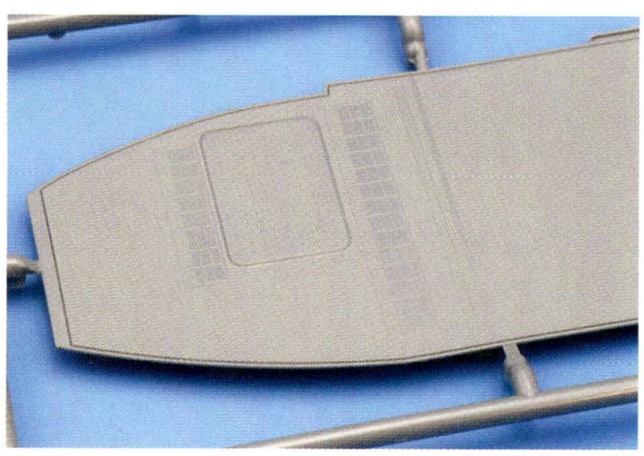

Out-of-the-box it will assemble into a superbly detailed model of the first *Kaga* configuration and aftermarket accessories really are not necessary. Fujimi once produced a dedicated set but that has now been long out of production.

FUJIMI ***KAGA*** (KIT #433622) AND ***KAGA*** FULL HULL (KIT #451893) 1:700 scale

The plastic parts in these two kits are identical and were first released in 2019. Like Fujimi's *Akagi* kits #433615 and #451303 the level of detail and their fineness is superlative and unlikely to be bettered by any injection moulded kit. The aircraft complement, AA guns, hatches and ready-use lockers are all included, and an inspection of the flight deck shows restrained planking lines that are scale-like. What is important is how these two kits differ. Kit #433622 is a standard waterline version and is notable for the four sheets of decals included. An extensive set of flight deck marking suitable for the Pearl Harbor Operation or Midway Sea Battle are provided. The remaining three sheets provide decals for the airwing. Besides the *hinomarus*, accurate fuselage and tailplane stripes for the aircraft *Kaga* carried, but also specific tail codes and any special markings some aircraft carried. Making the best use of these decals will take some research on your part because the instructions only show generic placement of markings on the aircraft.

The full hull version of the kit (#451893) includes a lower hull (with integrally moulded bilge keels), screws and shafts in red plastic, and a black plastic display stand. Note that several versions of this kit have also been released with different accessories. The present example included a fret of photoetched brass parts that replaces most of the support pillars with an open lattice work, flight deck netting, davits, companionway ladders, funnel foot ropes, and some catwalks. The etched parts are very fine, with the railings particularly so, and etched to length to fit specific areas of the ship. Photographic instructions show where each part goes. Other versions of the kit have included wooden deck overlays, or nothing but the plastic parts. The inclusions are not noted on the identical box lids but on a small sticker on the box end. Check before you buy. The other difference between the full hull and standard waterline version is the decal sheet. The full hull version contains a less extensive set of markings for the flight deck and only generic *hinomarus* for the airwing.

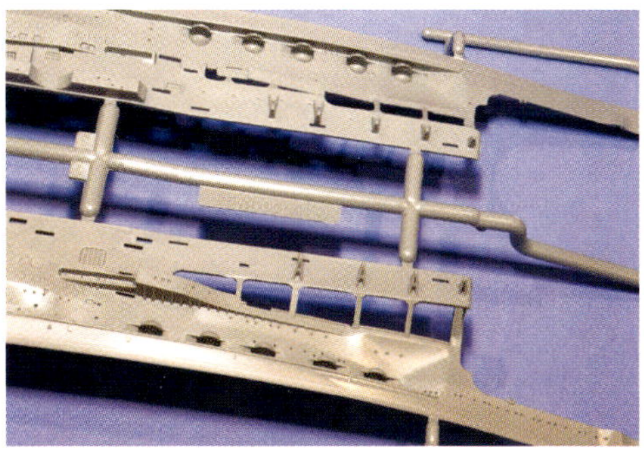

The fineness of the detail and complexity of the hull side moulding is remarkable for a small-scale ship kit.

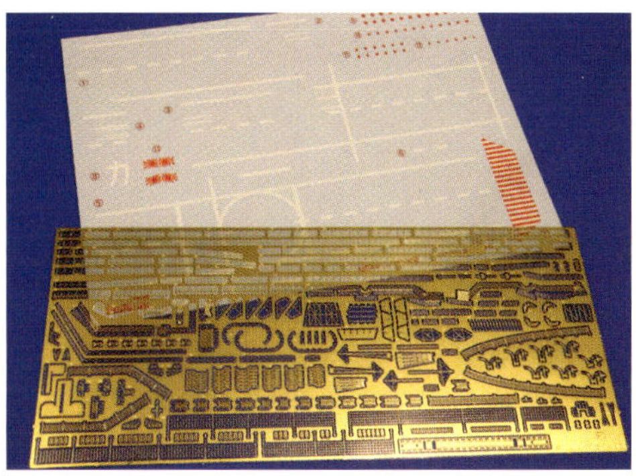

The etch brass detail set and simple decals included in this version of the full-hull kit. The etched parts are relief etched for added detail.

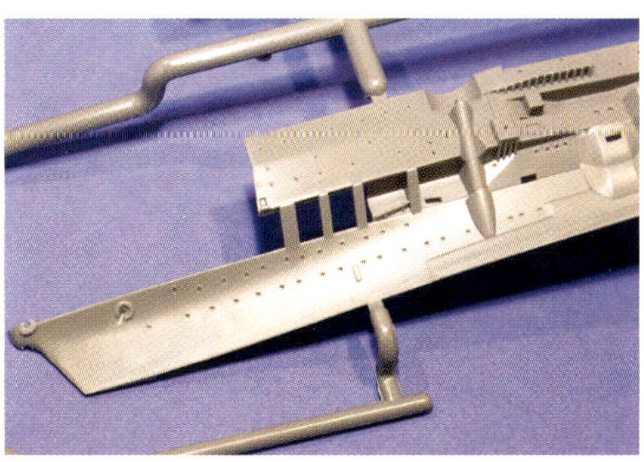

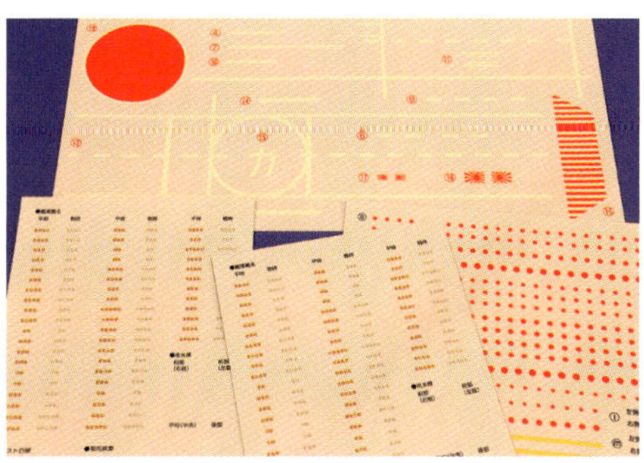

The extensive decal sheets included in the waterline version of the kit.

AOSHIMA JAPANESE CARRIER-BORNE AIRCRAFT TYPE 96 (KIT #059449)

1:700 scale

This confusingly named kit suggests that it contains one specific aircraft – a Type 96, usually interpreted as the Mitsubishi A5M4 (Allied code name 'Claude') but shows an Aichi D1A2 dive bomber and a B4Y1 torpedo plane as well. To clarify, in Japanese military nomenclature the number refers to the date the type went into production in the Japanese calendar, so *96* refers to the year 25*96*. The kit provides three sprues of two aircraft of the three types. The open cockpits are hollowed out, and the landing gear are provided as separate parts, but no torpedoes are included. The wings sport fine raised lines for ribs and panel lines but are marred by large moulding lugs representing the interplane and cabane struts. At the very least the interplane lugs should be removed and the cabane lugs reduced in thickness to a fine peg to allow the upper wing to be attached to the fuselage. The folded wings for the B4Y1 are included. A simple decal sheet of *hinomarus* and some generic fuselage stripes are provided. Despite the kit's limitations, it does provide a different deck load for *Kaga*'s operations in China and *Akagi*'s early operational years.

The moulded lugs for representing interplane struts are thick and an immediate improvement is made by simply cutting them away altogether. In 1:700 scale they are not missed because they would not be visible to the naked eye.

FUJIMI *KAGA* PREMIUM EDITION (KIT #600413)

1:350 scale

The largest plastic model of *Kaga* extant was first released in 2015 and has been re-released several times including different accessories. Versions of the kit have included a wooden deck overlay; hundreds of 1:350 sailors; and a Midway Sea Battle version that includes extra aircraft and a decal sheet to recreate every aircraft that she carried into battle, as well as the large flight deck *hinomaru*. The version shown here is the 'Premium Edition' that includes a large set of photoetched brass details. The sheets are extensive, covering the complicated under-deck lattice and support trusses, pre-measured railings, flight deck nettings, crash barriers, arresting cables and various supports, to name but a few. One fret is pre-coloured for the landing light system. Decals are included for the flight deck, but also a set of pre-cut masks in yellow so-called 'Kabuki' tape to paint yourself (where modellers came up with this ridiculous name is unknown to me; in Japan it is simply known as masking tape. To be clear, *kabuki* is a form of classical theatre). The flight deck decals and masks are those carried during the Pearl Harbor Operation.

The large plastic mouldings are superb

Crisply moulded detail is found throughout the kit.

and carry a great deal of detail. For a model this large and subject so complex, the part count is surprisingly low, ensuring straightforward assembly. The AA guns are assembled from detailed multiple parts, and the gun barrels appear very much in scale. None of the parts show any flash, mould seam lines, or sink marks. The flight deck shows neat and restrained planking detail, but the deck's tie-down points are omitted which is regrettable in this large scale. They can be indicated on the deck with some dark grey painted paper dots or decals punched using a miniature punch and die set. The airwing is comprised nine exquisitely detailed aircraft, three each of a Zero, Val and Kate. Panel lines are represented by petite recessed lines. The aircraft's delicate landing gear, propellers, and torpedoes are separate parts, as is the canopy. The canopy is moulded in grey and unfortunately not in clear plastic. However, a room temperature vulcanizing (RTV) rubber mould can be taken from the kit's canopy parts and cast in clear resin, which would really enhance realism.

This large-scale kit will provide a good basis for a fine model of *Kaga*. The instructions come in a booklet form with an extensive history and well-reproduced photos of the ship. Some minor refinements to the kit as noted here, and judicious use of after-market parts will elevate the finished model but even out-of-the-box the kit assembles into a detailed representation of this pioneering vessel.

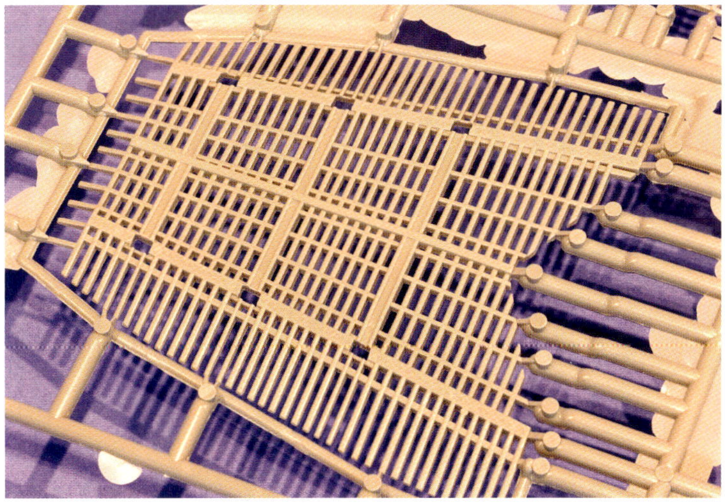

The moulded under-deck lattice work is remarkably fine given the limitations of injection moulded plastic.

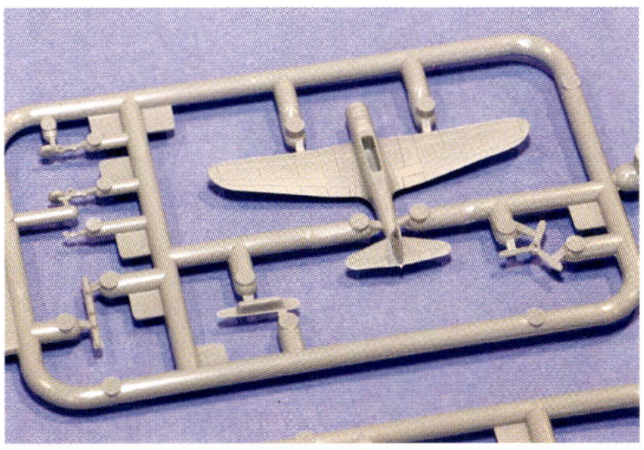

The detailing on the aircraft is very fine – just the heavily moulded propeller blades will need to be thinned down to match the finesse of the rest of the airframe.

The 'premium edition' comes with remarkable volume of detail accessory sets that when bundled as part of this kit yields the modeller substantial savings over having to source and purchase them individually.

HASEGAWA *AKAGI* (KIT #40025) AND (OPTIONAL) DETAILS SETS A (KIT #72126), B (KIT #72127), C (KIT #72128) AND WOODEN DECK STICKER (KIT #72125) 1:350 scale

Representing the ship in 1941, Hasegawa's kit is the most detailed carrier kit available. The main hull castings are amply detailed with plating lines, footropes, and scuttles with rigols. The flight deck planking is well done, but unfortunately show no aircraft tie down points. Underneath the flight deck the trusses and beams are effectively represented by crisply moulded grids. Overall, the level of surface detail is superior to Fujimi's 1:350 *Kaga* mouldings. Again, the extensive bridge splinter padding is missing and will have to be made from two-part epoxy putty by the modeller. The kit includes an extensive decal sheet for the airwing with tail codes, stripes and *hinomarus* for the Pearl Harbor Operation. The aircraft themselves are moulded in clear plastic. The flight deck markings are provided as decals, but Hasegawa also includes a paper flag sheet and two special flags that signal the ship is ready to launch aircraft or receive them. Fine blackened chain is provided for the anchors. The kit has also been released as a Midway Sea Battle version, although the flight deck decals for that version are included on the sheet for the 1941 version.

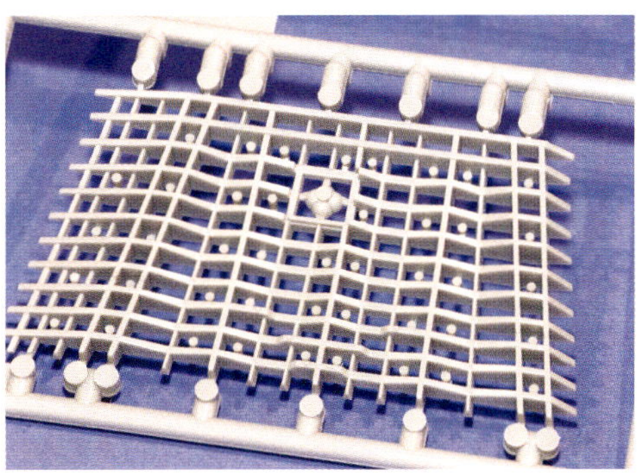

The lattice under the flight deck is a little heavy and highlights the value of the photoetch lattice work in this larger scale.

The *Akagi* kit was first released in 2008 and since then a large assortment of after-

The kit box with optional detail sets. There are further sets in plastic which one can add that increases the size of the airwing and provides more of the ship's small boats.

market accessories has been released for it. The sets feature etched metal trusswork under the flight deck, hatch and door details, foot ropes, railings – and the options go on and on. Several 3D printed accessories from various manufacturers offer a new bridge (with and without splinter netting), masts and yards, better detailed AA guns, Carley floats and ship's boats. These sets go in and out of production, so what is available at any given time is quite variable. Hasegawa released four sets of aftermarket parts that have been in continuous production and generally available. These sets provide updated *basic* detailing, so that it *builds upon* what is included in the kit instead of replacing the plastic parts with more detailed (but not always) parts. Set A focuses on railings for specific areas of the ship, and the many different types of companionway ladders and stairs. Set B concentrates on the flight deck with complete flight deck netting, propeller thrust guards, crash barriers and under deck rail system featured. Set C provides boat chocks, oars to place into the ship's boats, and airscrews for the aircraft. Don't forget to twist the airscrew blades slightly before fixing to the nose. The wooden deck set provided beautifully laser-etched deck planks as close to 1:350 as possible on virtually grain free wood veneer. A small etched brass sheet provides the shapes of the elevator to paint and fix to the wood veneer for a clean finish. Dry transfers are provided for the deck markings, and as noted earlier, another option is to have a paint mask made.

The value of the Hasegawa detail sets is that what they include is sensible and does not replace items for the sake of replacing items and synergistically enhances the kit contents to yield a highly detailed and realistic model of the ship.

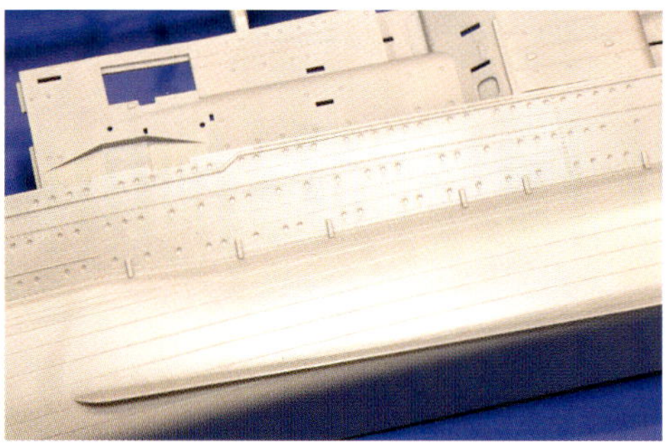

The plating detail is a little suspect being represented by fine recessed lines as opposed to the 'in and out' style of actual strakes of steel hull plating. The 'out' strakes can be represented with thin styrene sheet glued to every other strake, and butt ends scribed.

DEAGOSTINI *AKAGI* 1:250 scale

In 2017, the magazine publisher DeAgostini (USA) released the largest kit of *Akagi* extant. This is a multimedia kit composed of cast zinc, laser-cut wood, etched brass, and plastic components. Each month for a year a subscriber receives

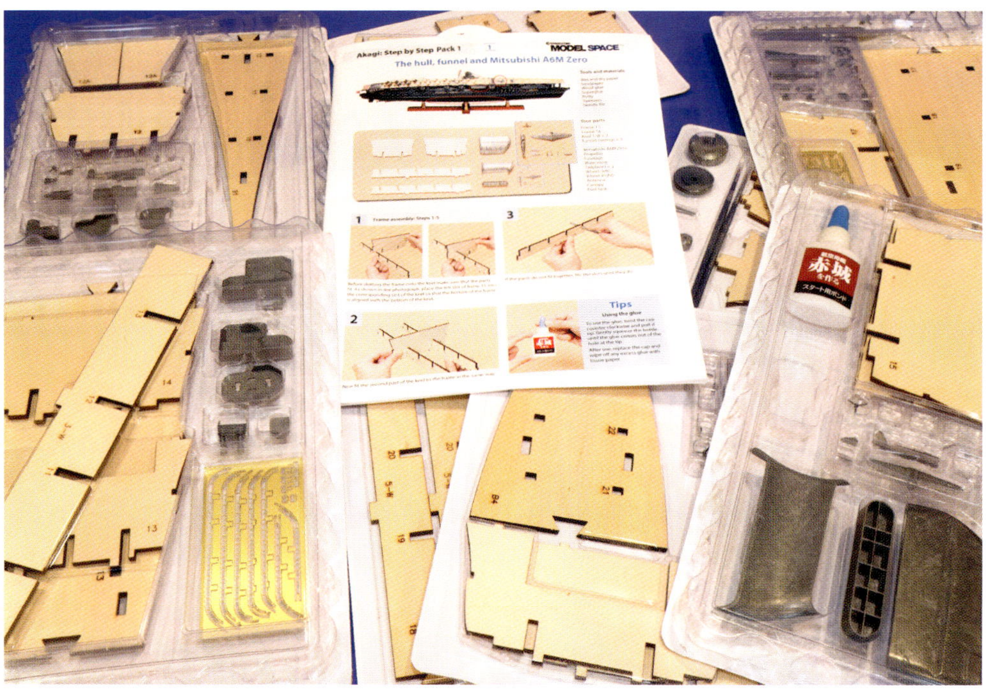

Being able to work comfortably in wood, metal, plastic and etched brass is a must for this kit. For the radio-control modeller, the wooden hull parts can be traced and scaled up to create a hull large enough to accommodate motors and speed controls. Scaling up the parts to 1:72 would allow conventional plastic kits to be used for the airwing.

a set of components and a fully illustrated instruction booklet showing the construction of the model. Laser-cut wood formers are glued together to form the hull, and this is planked over with strips of wood and shaped with sandpaper. Metal parts provide items like the bridge and all ship's guns, boats, aircraft and fittings, and fine wood strips to plank the flight deck. Railings and flight deck trusses, decks with treadplate detail are etched brass. It builds into an extraordinary model that is well detailed on its own, but the dedicated modeller can find many small details to add. The kit appears to be produced in Spain and is not readily available now but can be had from internet auction sites.

This model should not be confused with the 1:250 *Akagi* model from DeAgostini Japan. The Japanese partwork ran for 100 weeks and each instalment provided a few parts and detailed booklet covering history and assembly of the ship. However, the Japanese model was not a conventional model kit *per se*, but a set of pre-painted or coloured plastic and metal parts that were assembled with screws or glue. Prefabrication was done to such an extent that several working gimmicks were incorporated into the model, such as anchors that can be raised or lowered, screws that turned, and search and navigation lights that lit up. These and other functions were operated by the buttons of a remote-control unit. Despite its toylike functionality and appeal, the model is remarkably realistic and well detailed. There is no doubt that the Japanese and USA kits share parts in common., but this version was only offered in Japan. It is no longer available but whole sets or individual instalments are available on internet auction sites or sometimes in Japan at second-hand book shops in major Japanese cities like Tokyo's Jimbocho or Shimbashi areas.

HASEGAWA ZERO FIGHTER TYPE 21 & CARRIER DIVE-BOMBER MODEL 11 & TYPE 97 ATTACK-BOMBER MODEL 3 'PEARL HARBOR ATTACK'

(KIT # SP348) 1:48 scale

Kaga and *Akagi's* airwing at Pearl Harbor (8 December 1941, JST) is spectacularly represented by Hasegawa's 2016 special edition kit. The large box includes three complete kits of a Zero, Val, and Kate. The aircraft kits are well-regarded and feature fine detail, accurate outlines, and crystal-clear canopies. The details of the kit cockpits are a little simplified, as are the visible radial engines but detailed enough from what can be seen through the cockpit and cowlings. Panel detail is fine recessed lines and breakdown of the parts ensures easy assembly. The star of the kit is the huge and perfectly printed decal sheet and instruction sheets that provides two markings and finishing details for two schemes for each aircraft. For the Zero, schemes for an aircraft of the second attack wave from *Akagi* (A1-102) and *Kaga* (AII-168); the Kates from the first attack wave from *Akagi* and *Hiryu*; and a Val from *Akagi*'s second attack wave (AI-203), and a second wave attack aircraft from *Kaga* (AII-256) are provided. Hasegawa notes that the aircraft drawings provided are reduced to 70% on the side elevations and 40% for plan views which can be scaled up to assist the modeller precisely locating decals and anti-glare panels by scaling up the drawings.

BORDER *AKAGI* BRIDGE WITH FLIGHT DECK AND NAKAJIMA B5N2 'KATE' (KIT #BSF 001) 1:35 scale

This remarkable kit builds into a large diorama of *Akagi's* bridge on a section of flight deck with a Type 97 'Kate' carrier attack plane. The box is filled to the brim with well moulded parts. The bridge itself is composed of a few large mouldings. Details to be added include Lewis guns, speaking tubes, binoculars, compan-

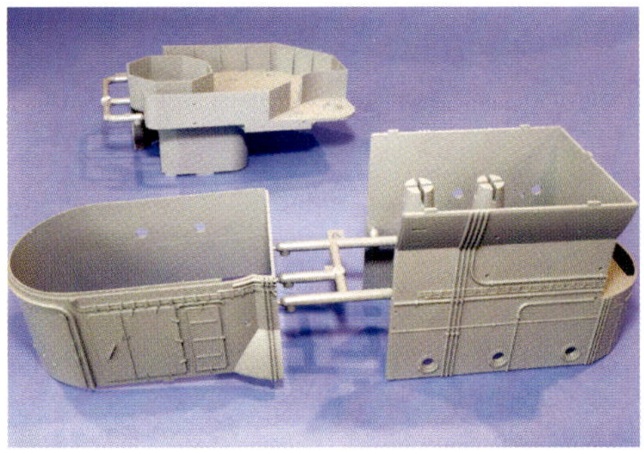

ionway stairs, and all the equipment found on the bridge. Clear plastic inserts provide porthole glazing. The diorama was clearly inspired by photos of the bridge with battle ensigns flying on the way to Pearl Harbor. The parts are fairly well detailed but are a little plain in missing prominent weld marks and rivet lines. Perhaps a lot of the small surface details were left off because much of the bridge structure is covered with long tubes of splinter matting that would cover such detail. The plainness of the major parts can also be relieved by careful shading and weathering. The mast is composed of several plastic parts that are thin enough to be pulled out of true by the strain of rigging and best replaced with brass rod. The thin yardarm sports moulded block detail to reeve the signal halyards but they do not look realistic. In this large scale, individual metal blocks should be procured from vendors that sell rigging supplies for wooden sailing ship models. The main navigation light above the rangefinder can be lit and the kit provides the electrical components and switch to do so. The flight deck is glued up from several sections. The planking detail has a simulated woodgrain finish that will either delight or annoy modellers, and the aircraft tie-down points are moulded into the planks, to which etched brass tie-down points are fixed. In this large scale, planking the deck with real wood strips or a veneer would be far more realistic. The decal sheets provide flags and some chalk details of the Pearl Harbor Operation. Decal flags on their own are fragile, and best fixed to some aluminium foil and shaped before tying to the halyards. Another option is to replace the flags with real cloth items usually used by RC model ship builders.

The Type 97 aircraft is fully detailed inside and out. One standout feature is that Border moulded-in stressed wing and fuselage panels. Decal markings are provided for Lt Col Fuchida Mitsuo, whose aircraft code was AI-301, or Major Murata Shigaharu's aircraft coded AI-311. Surprisingly, the decals are quite simple, consisting in the main of *hinomarus* and codes, but no stencils. The aircraft mounted to the base would be quite a sight except for the lack of figures. No figures of deck crew, aircrew or officers are included. This is a pity because without them the diorama resembles a *Mary Celeste*. The only figures available are expensive 3D printed aftermarket items. The scale chosen also means that only 1:35 scale aircraft can be fitted to the deck, for which there is only one alternative kit of a A6M2 Zero also offered by Border. The flight deck kit can be purchased without any aircraft or bundled in with the Type 97 as shown here, or with a A6M2 Zero. Overall, the kit provides the basis for a stunning diorama, but a lot of engrossing detail work by the modeller is the only way to bring the scene to life.

A view of the wing's underside that shows remarkably realistic but understated stressed skin detailing. This 'oil canning' effect is reproduced all over the airframe and careful painting and shading will make it stand out.

BORDER *AKAGI* BRIDGE WITH FLIGHT DECK

(KIT #BELT 72002) 1:72 scale

This kit is not just scaled down version of the 1:35 kit whose part breakdown is quite different in places. The primary bridge structure parts are in two halves, and the flight deck is supplied in one piece. The bridge fittings sport basic detail, but as in the larger kit small details like weld marks and rivets are missing. The flight deck planks are defined by recessed lines with the aircraft tie down points moulded into the plank runs devoid of any wood-graining detail. No provision for illuminating the bridge signal lights is provided, and again, the masts and yard are flimsy and will need to be replaced with spars soldered up from brass rod for strength. No figures are provided, but in this popular scale some could be taken from other aircraft and military miniature kits and converted to look like Japanese sailors. Aftermarket 3D printed figures are available in this scale from the likes of Triumph Model of China.

This kit is by Border and is marketed in different countries under different names. The kit shown here is from Japan and sold under the Beaver Corporation brand and includes a bonus 1:16 figure of a Japanese

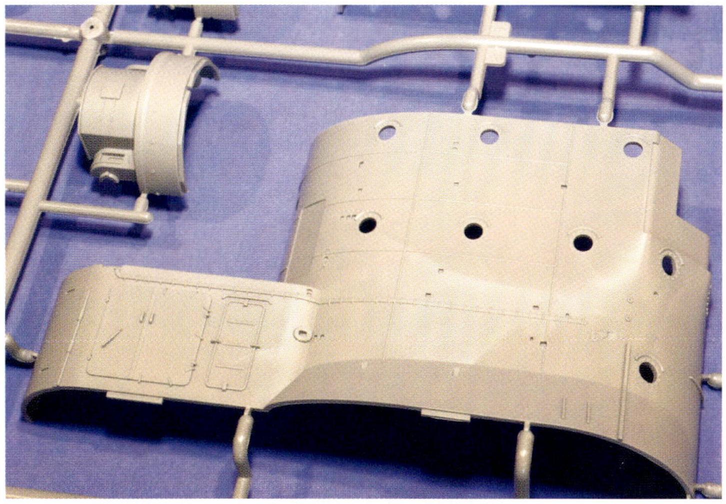

naval officer who looks like Admiral Yamamoto who devised the raid and led it on *Akagi*, although not named as such on the box or in the kit. With the diorama in 1:72, any aircraft carried by *Akagi* after her modernization can be set upon the deck. Finding 1:72 kits of a Zero, Kate, or Val from the likes of Tamiya, Hasegawa, Airfix, and Fujimi is no problem and the biggest task for the modeller is re-creating the markings they carried when attached to *Akagi*. This kit can be turned into an amazing diorama by fitting lights to the bridge and electric motors to the aircraft to spin the propellers to recreate that moment the raid on Pearl Harbor commenced.

BORDER IJN CARRIER CREW PILOTS & OFFICERS
(KIT #BR-006) 1:35 scale

This set of eight resin figures was designed to go with the *Akagi* bridge and flight deck set. The figures will provide a sense of scale, and some life to a completed diorama. However, this set alone will not convey the dynamism of the moment the planes were launched at Pearl Harbor. The photos of the moment show the deck and certainly the bridge much busier, full of crewmen, officers, and lookouts. The deck was abuzz with crew readying planes, pilots waiting to board, and when they started to take off, the deck was lined with the entire deck crew waving and wishing the pilots well in that typically Japanese way. The figures themselves are well cast and detailed, but they show a great deal of sameness. This is likely caused by the figures beings sculpted by 3D modelling using the same base rendering. The facial expressions and features show little variation, and the body shapes are all tall and slender. To add the dynamism and excitement of that moment in history, and normal variation in human physique, figures from other ranges should be added to supplement this set. Alternative figures were released by Triumph Model from China who offer a large set of 1:35 (and 1:72) crew for

The figures have an unattractive sameness to them that resembles a mannequin.

the dioramas which can be purchased as a complete set or individually.

ACCESSORIES

TETRA MODELWORKS *AKAGI* FLIGHT DECK SET FOR HASEGAWA (KIT #70003) 1:700 scale

This is just one of many aftermarket accessory sets for *Akagi* and *Kaga* in 1:700. A set for *Akagi* is included here to give an idea of how complex these sets are. This flight deck set provides laser-etched wooden veneer overlay for the flight deck, but also all the truss-and-beams work supporting the deck. All the trusses are open lattices, and they attach to the underside of a fully detailed etched steel deck. The wooden overlay is fixed to the top and is enhanced by fully detailed arrestor wire sets and crash barriers. No markings are provided, and you can use the kit decals if you seal the wood first with some gloss varnish or use the kit decals to make a stencil and paint. The set is complicated, and the use of fine tweezers and a magnifier is a must. A page from the instructions shows how complicated assembling this set will be. It is, like many of the aftermarket sets extant, only for the modeller who must have everything.

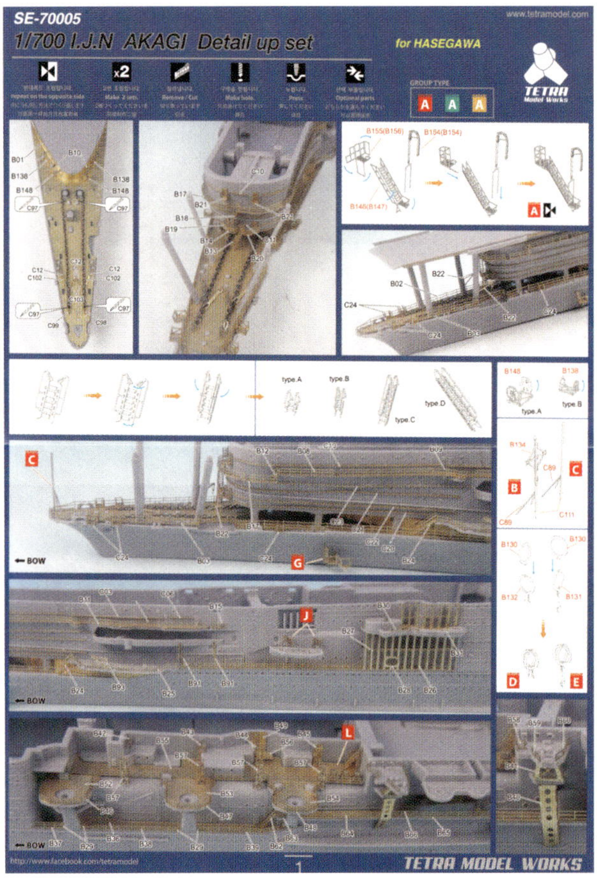

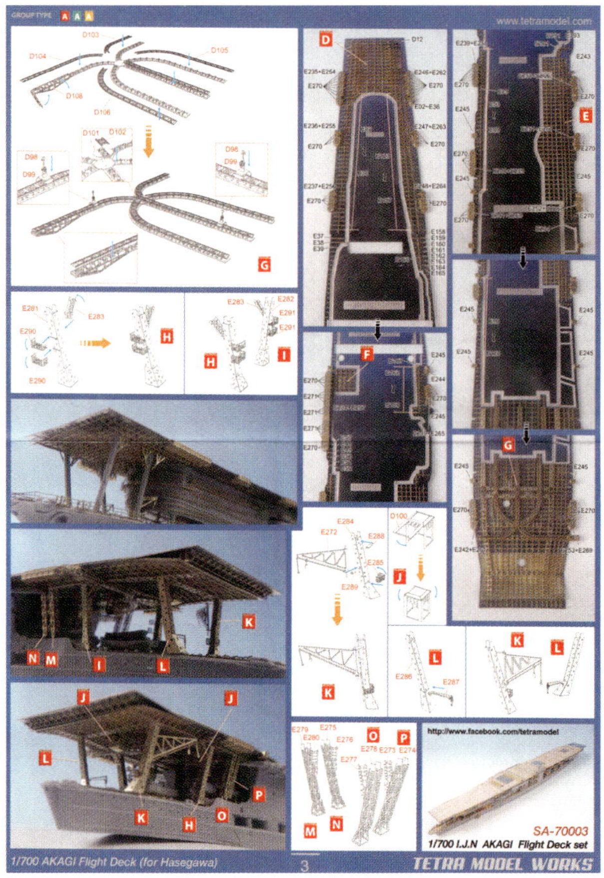

Keen eyesight and steady hands are required to assemble this set.

FINEMOLDS NANO DREAD ACCESSORIES FOR JAPANESE NAVY WARSHIPS 1:700 scale

This company has been releasing an ever-increasing range of generic warship detailing parts in injection moulded plastic. The parts are extremely tiny, and carry full detail including latches, hinges, and locks. The details are as good

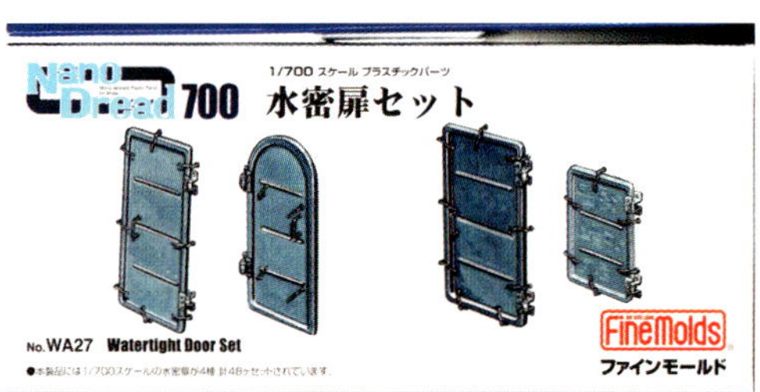

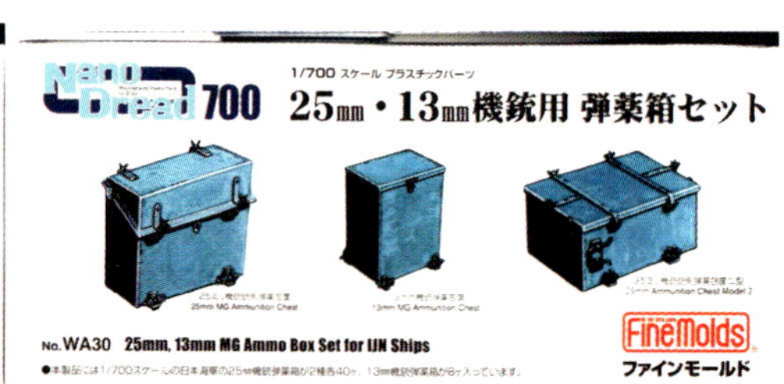

as any etched brass accessory with the advantage of being in styrene plastic so are easy to add to a model with no more than ordinary plastic cement. Shown are three sets useful for *Akagi* and *Kaga*, with the latest set providing the splinter padding. A wide range of sets that include super detailed davits, ship's boats, radars, and armaments are also available. The parts are so tiny that care will have to be taken when removing them from the sprue lest they fly off into the great abyss of the workshop floor, never to be seen again.

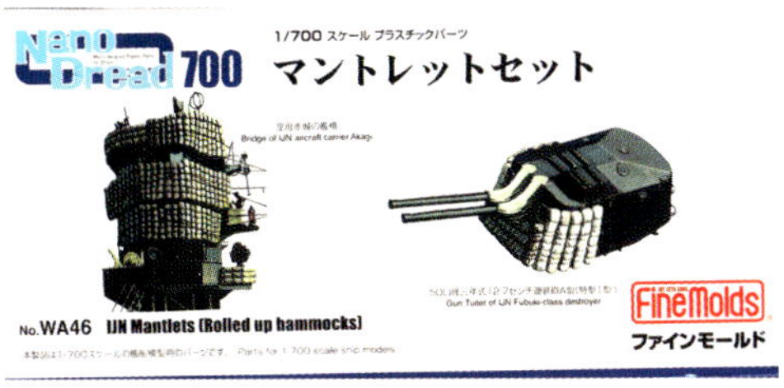

BUNKER STUDIO 3D PRINTED ACCESSORY SETS FOR *AKAGI*

1:700 scale

A remarkable set of 3D printed accessories for *Akagi* is available that provides enhanced details over the kit parts but also simplifies assembly. Whole units of the ship, like the bridge, are printed in one piece, and the printing lines are so fine they cannot be seen and disappear under a coat of paint. Once the parts are carefully snipped from the printing cages they can be fixed to the model without any additional preparation. Any items that cannot be printed are provided on a small etched brass set. Beyond those sets dedicated to *Akagi*, this company offers a wide range of generic Japanese Navy fittings useable for any ship. The effectiveness of the sets is seen in Mr Douglas Chan's build of the *Akagi* in the Modemakers' Showcase.

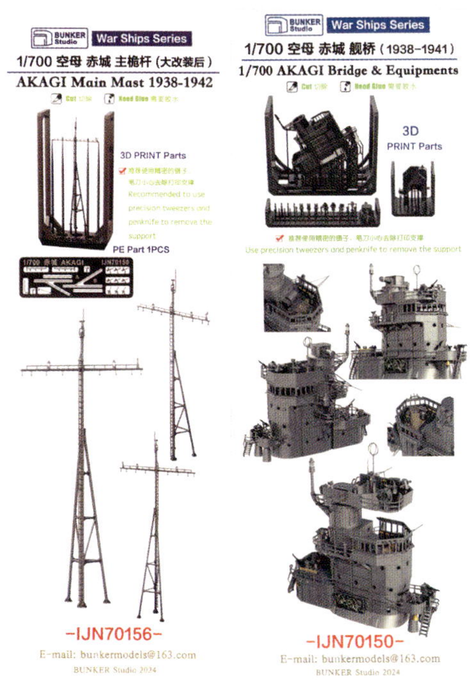

Care must be taken when removing the mast from its moulding cages because resin is quite brittle. Rigging will also require care to avoid stressing the part lest it bends and snaps.

BUILDING FUJIMI 1:700 AIRCRAFT CARRIER *AKAGI* & *KAGA*

Published by Kaiga, Tokyo

A visit to any model shop in Japan or online retailer will have an extensive book section showing how to build and detail a particular kit. The Kaiga book is one of a series that has expert plastic modellers in Japan demonstrate how to build Fujimi's *Akagi* and *Kaga*. In full colour, all the accessories and modifications to each kit are shown. In this edition, it is not just about adding detail, but also how the interior hangar decks can be built from scratch from sheet styrene. The aforementioned Nano Dread parts feature heavily in the builds, and interestingly, items like photoetched railings are omitted because they are considered far out-of-scale. The text is entirely in Japanese and many of the products used such as adhesives and paints are not readily available outside of Japan. However, the author has tested translation apps on the text, and a reasonably comprehensible English translation was obtained.

Modelmakers' Showcase

HASEGAWA *AKAGI* 1:700 scale

By DOUGLAS CHAN

Mr Chan from Hong Kong pulled out all the stops on his build of Hasegawa's *Akagi*. Extensive photoetch details were added, such as Tetra Modelworks etch set and all the Bunker Studio resin 3D printed accessories for this ship. Much to his surprise, he noted that the extensive photoetched underdeck deck lattice work was unexpectedly straightforward to attach, but the especially difficult and nerve-wracking operation was mating the flight deck with all its lattice work to the hull. He reports that the use of the 3D printed parts greatly simplified the detailing and made for a 'tedium free' build by not having to modify the kit parts. Careful painting and weathering brings out the details of this outstanding model.

The photoetched details and 3D printed parts give the model a crisp and defined appearance so important in small scale models like this.

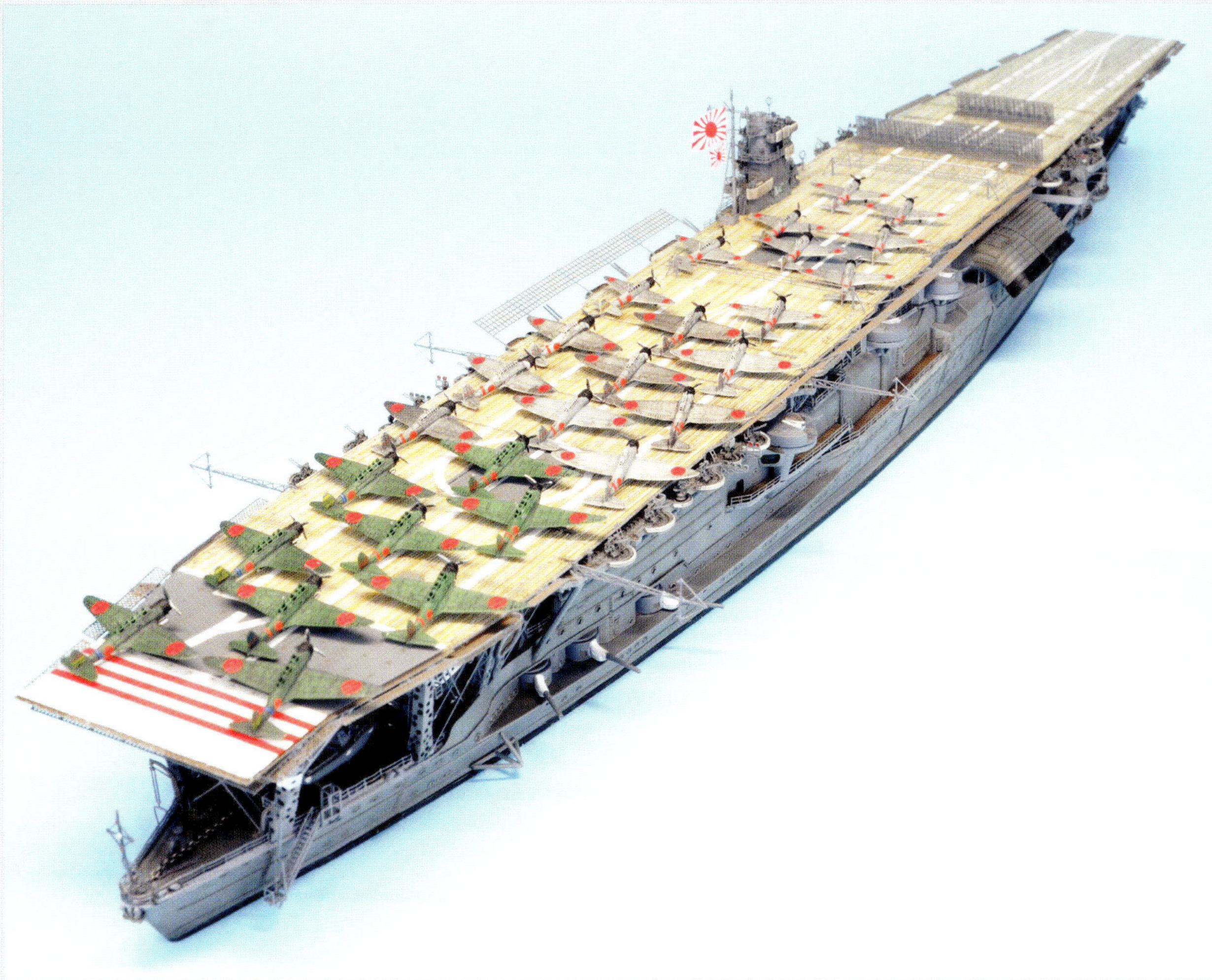

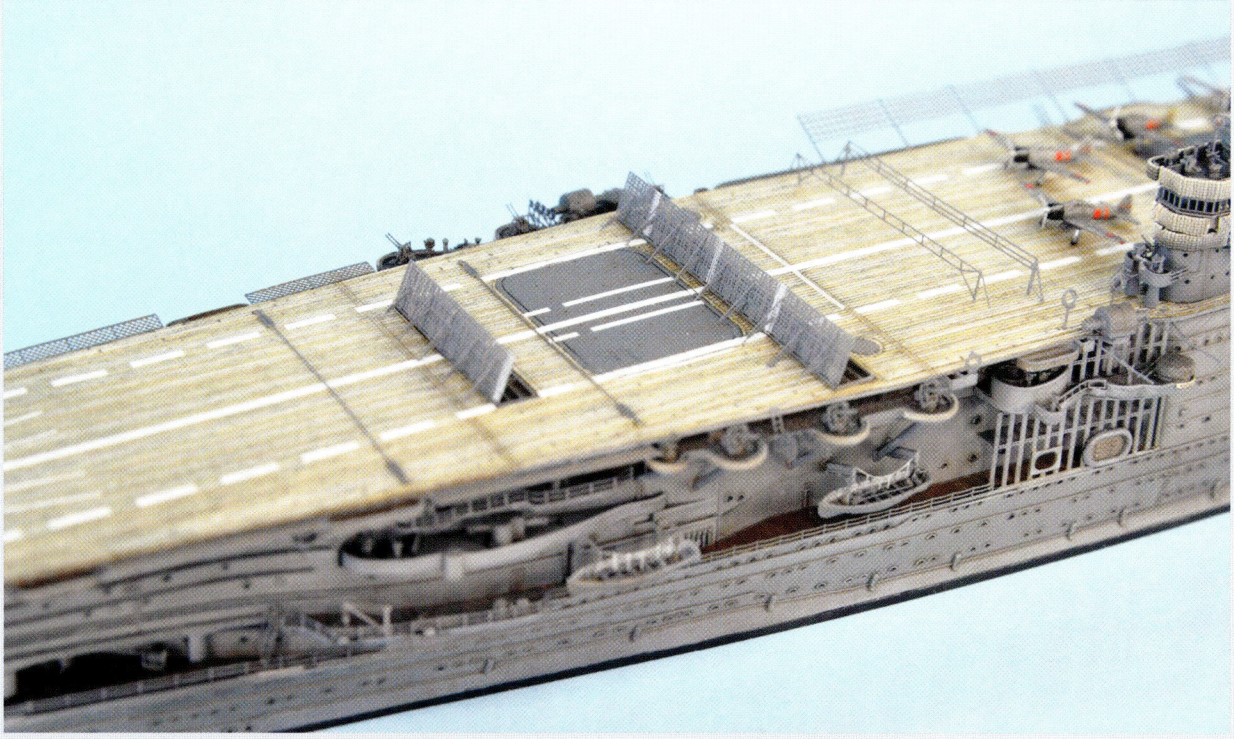

The wooden decking is extremely realistic giving the impression that individual planks of slightly different wood shade colour have been laid.

FUJIMI *KAGA* 1:350 scale

By DO TRUONG SA

Mr Sa hails for Hanoi, Vietnam. His father's service in the Vietnamese Navy sparked his interest in model ships when he was a schoolboy and he became a serious modeller at 19. He says that his build of Fujimi's *Kaga* was one of his proudest achievements, taking three months to complete but the research took two years of planning, gathering materials and researching in books, old archives, and watching Japanese videos of the wartime IJN. His superlative model made use of photoetched accessories, plenty of scratch building, and skilful painting and weathering to brings this most impressive model to life.

The addition of crewmen brings the model to life. The figures are carefully placed in groups to tell a story. Some are arming the aircraft; and the pilots are being briefed, for example. Others are working on an aircraft engine, and another group on the deck pushing a Val into position on the flight deck. There are no crew members that are standing around listlessly.

The careful weathering includes a line of green algae at the waterline so characteristic of a ship that has spent a long time at sea. Details like this, as well as guano droppings, are often missed.

FUJIMI *KAGA* 'THREE TIER FLIGHT DECK' 1:700 scale

By KERRY JANG

The two previous Modelmakers' Showcase models heavily modified the basic plastic kits with extensive scratchbuilt details and aftermarket accessory sets. In contrast, this 1:700 Fujimi kit of the three-decked *Kaga* was built out-of-the-box to see what could be achieved with just basic modelling skills to refine a few areas by drilling out lightening holes, careful assembly, and painting and shading. The ship itself was straightforward to assemble but requiring extensive pre-painting and shading of the decks as each is constructed and fixed to the hull over the top of the previous one. The airwing provided in the kits is just six aircraft, and they feature moulded struts and rigging, airscrew and undercarriage that is thick, clunky, and incredibly fiddly to fit. In this small scale, these parts are not visible and best left off, just adding some stubs fashioned from styrene card as makeshift landing gear. Straight out of the box, the kit builds into a fine replica of the ship, and what becomes apparent is how large her hull length funnels were and the consequent discomfort the heat must have been.

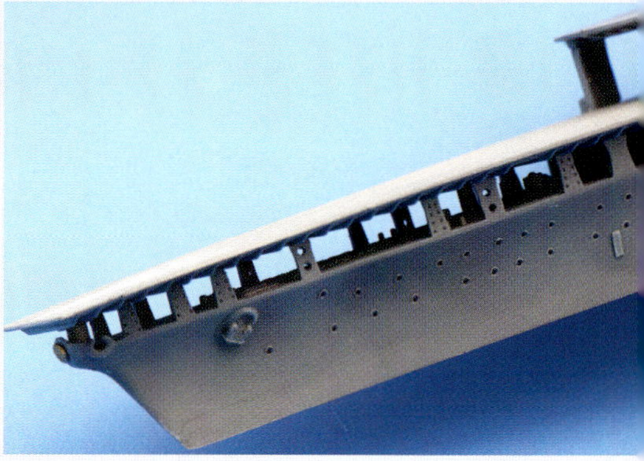

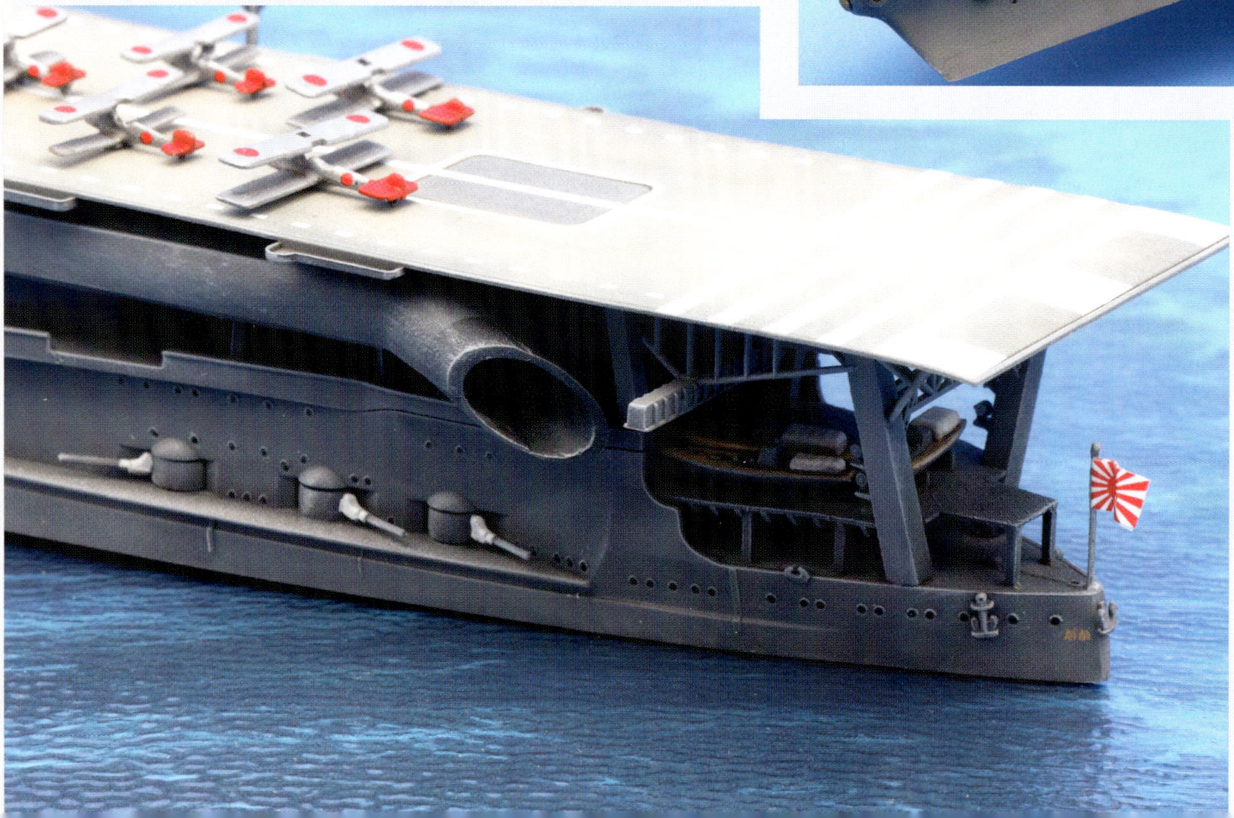

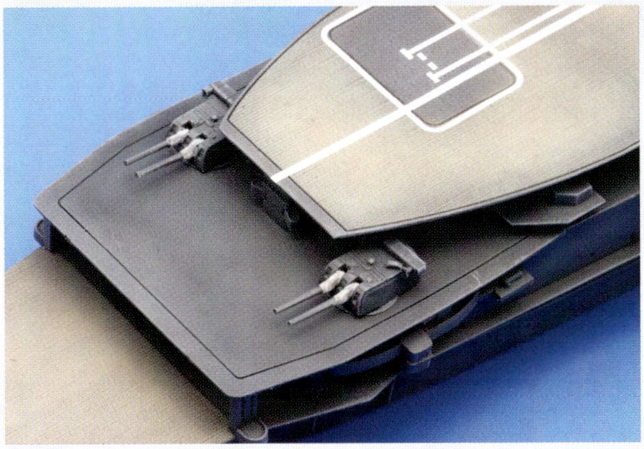

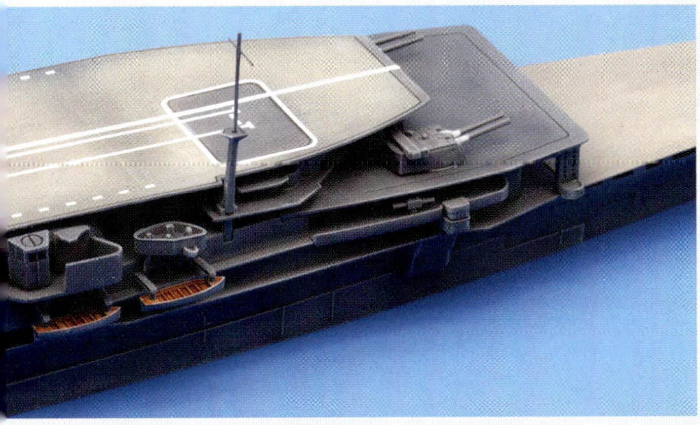

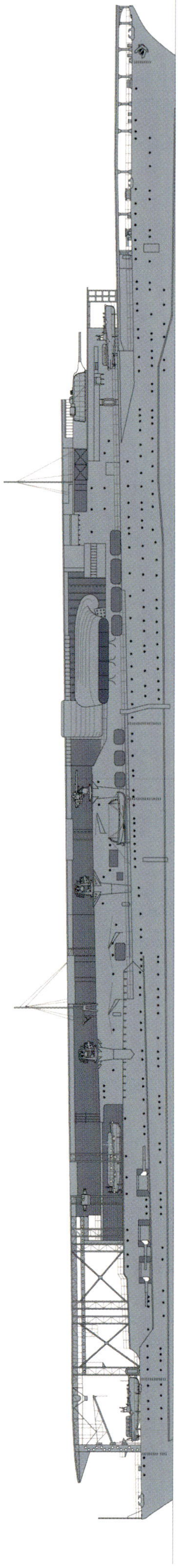

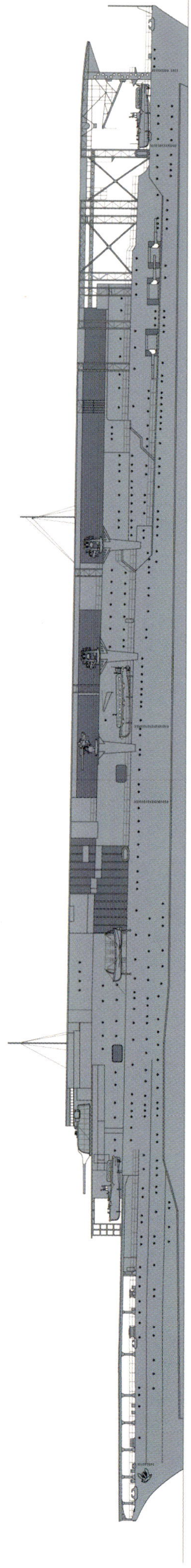

Akagi 1929

Akagi's colour scheme in 1929 was an overall blue grey. Over the years, photographs of her flight deck markings showed minor variations. The rays of the wind direction arrows were spaced differently, and the white markings right aft on the flight deck could have been different colours, such as red or yellow. It is thought the colour changed to help pilots identify their ship, or that the visibility of each colour to the pilots was being trialled.

Akagi 1941

The *Akagi* would have been painted in 'wartime painting colour' which was a dark grey with a slight blue tinge that she wore throughout her life. At the Midway Ocean Battle, *Akagi*'s forward flight deck carried a wide white band with a large *hinomaru* across the width of the deck.

Whether the marking was permanently painted or temporary remains controversial. The profile has been rendered in wartime painting colour, but the colour slightly adjusted to allow the details of the drawing to be more readily seen. The mix for the actual colour is provided in the text.

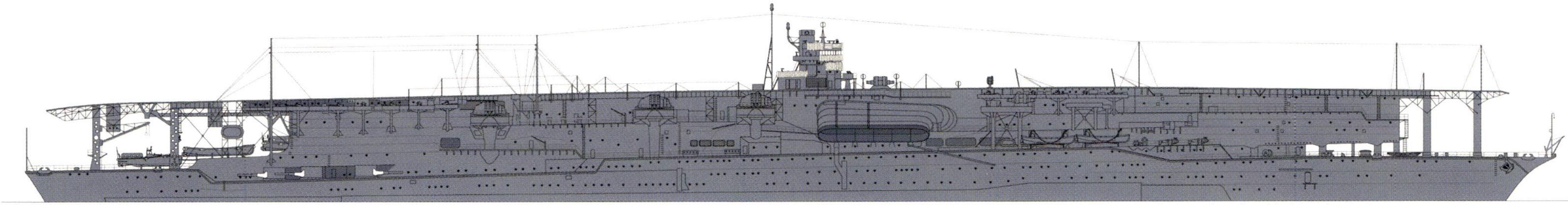

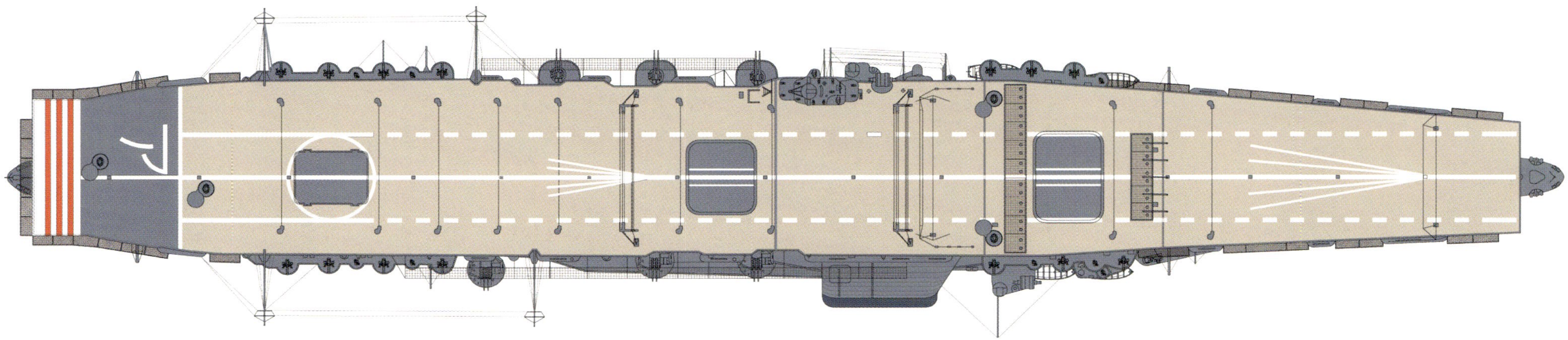

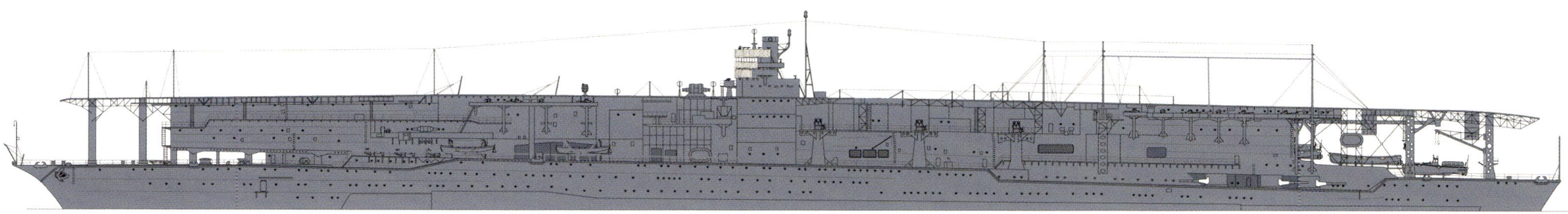

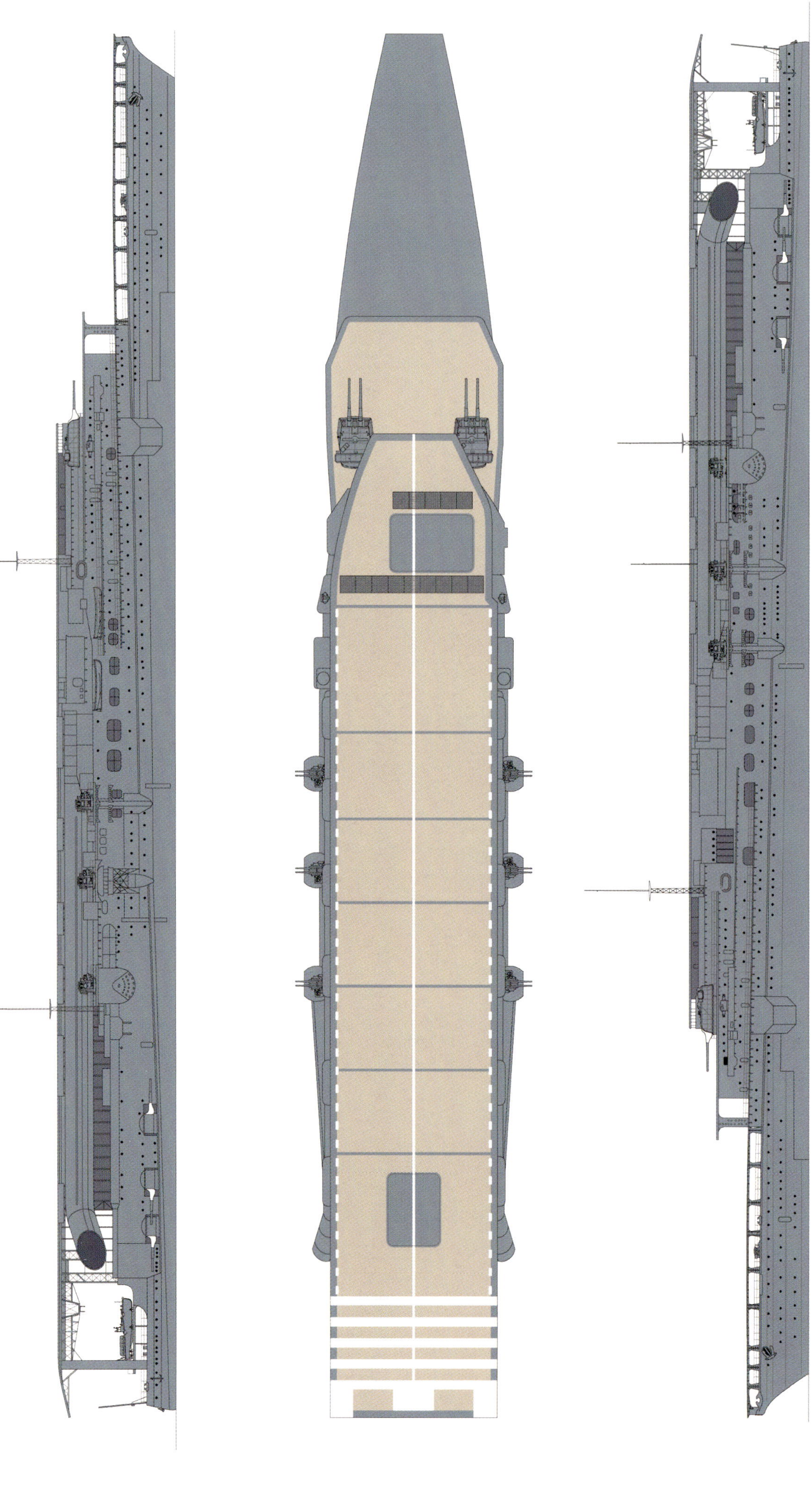

Kaga 1929
Kaga's overall all blue grey colour scheme in 1929.
The same minor changes to *Akagi's* deck colours also apply to *Kaga*.

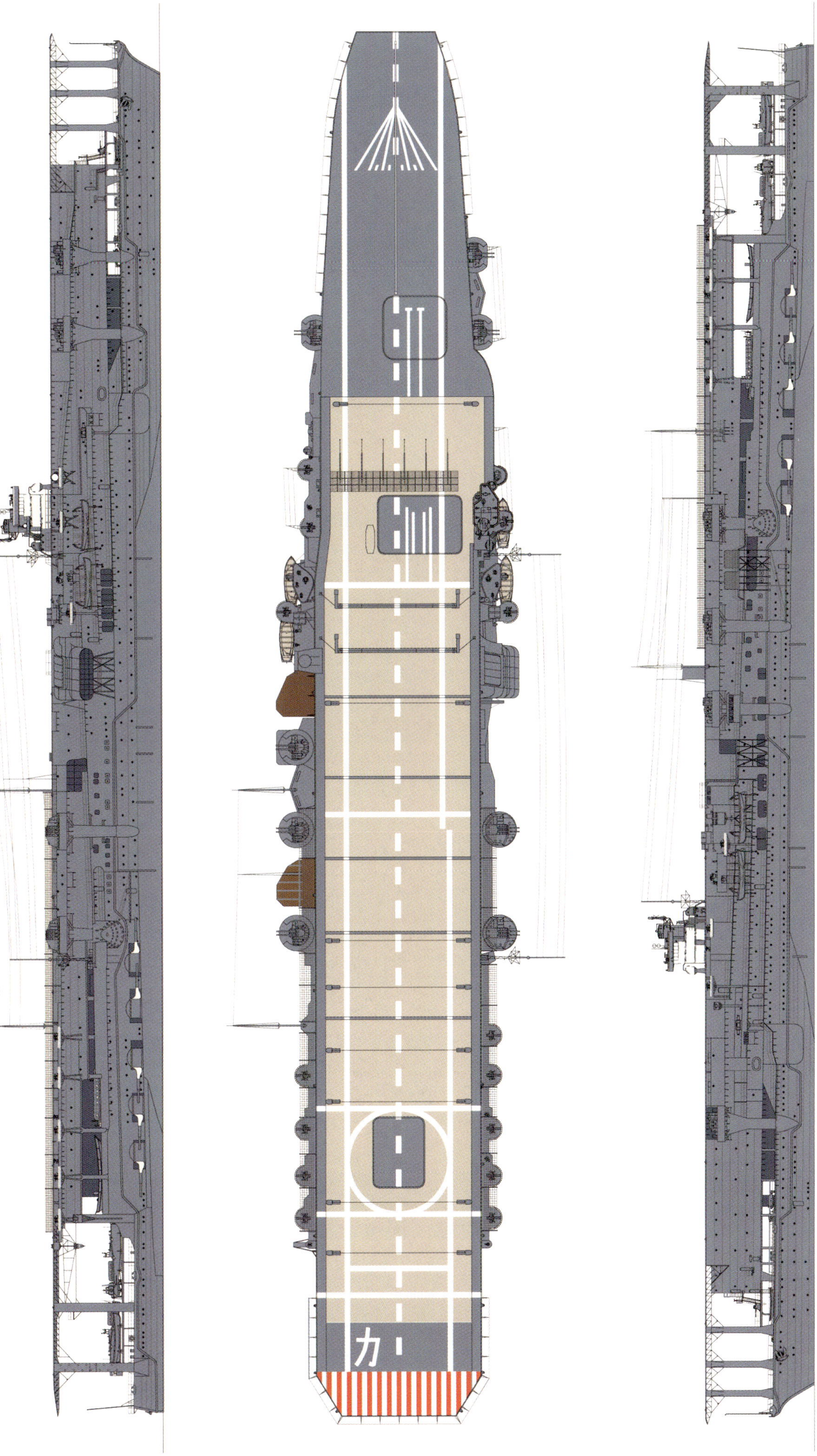

Kaga **1941**
Like *Akagi*, *Kaga* sported a 'wartime painting colour' finish. At Midway Ocean Battle, *Kaga* carried a large white outlined *hinomaru* on the forward flight deck.

Nakajima A1N & A1N2
The Nakajima A1N (top) was a Japanese-built version of the Gloster Gambet fighter that started production in 1929 and was also known as the Navy Type 3 Carrier Fighter. Fifty aircraft were built and powered by a Nakajima-built Bristol Jupiter engine. The A1N2 (bottom) used the Nakajima Kotobuki 2 engine and series production was started in 1930 with approximately 100 examples completed by 1932.

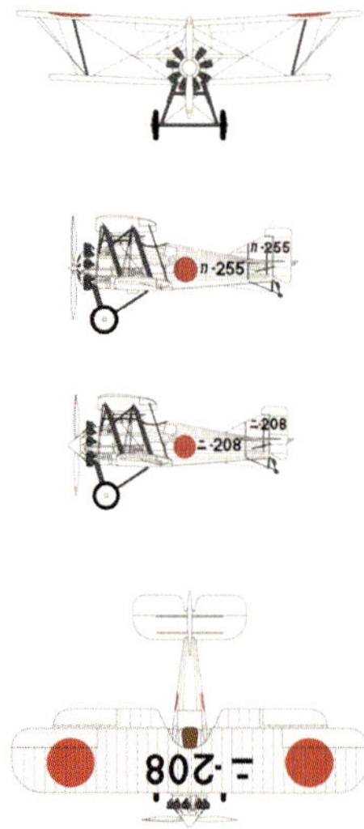

Aichi D3A1 Val
The Aichi D3A1 or Type 99 Carrier Bomber (Allied code name 'Val') was the primary dive bomber carried by *Akagi* and *Kaga*. Starting with the attack on Pearl Harbor, the D3A1 took part in all major Japanese carrier operations in the first ten months of the war.

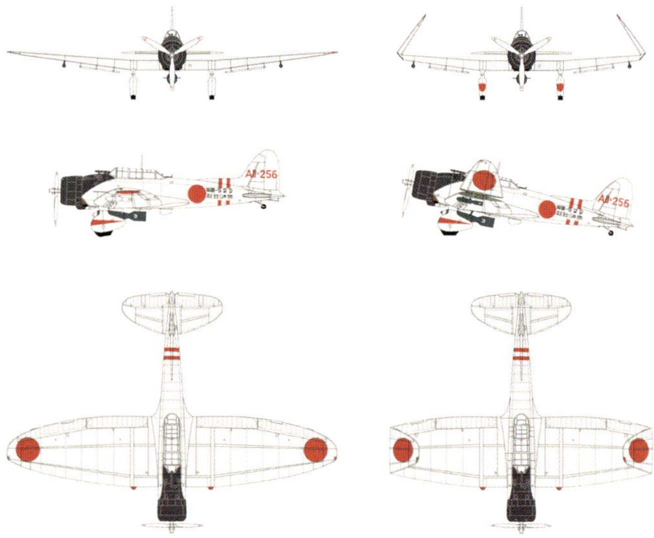

Nakajima A2N
The A2N1 was originally developed as a private venture by Nakajima. The A2N1, also designated the Type 90 Carrier Fighter was powered by a Nakajima Kotobuki 2 engine. The aircraft was approved for series production in April 1932. Approximately 100 were built, and a two-seat training version was developed (A3N) of which nearly 70 were built.

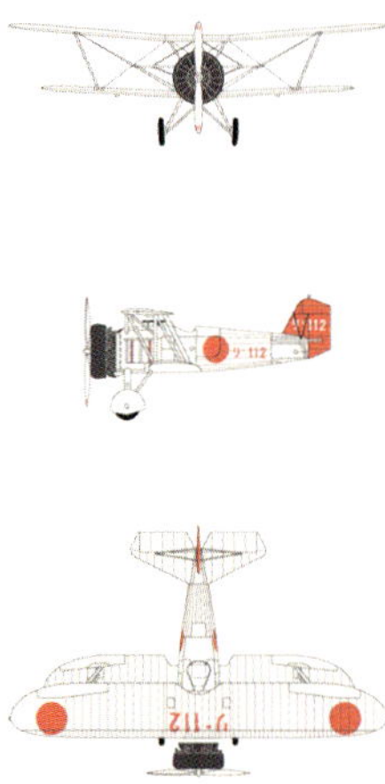

Mitsubishi A6M2b Zero
The Mitsubishi A6M2b Model 21 was also known as the Navy Fighter Type 0 (hence known unofficially as the 'Zero' instead of its official Allied code name 'Zeke'). The carrier-borne Model 21 combined excellent manoeuvrability, high airspeed, strong firepower and very long range of over 2600km. This endurance allowed it to range farther from its carrier than expected, appearing over distant battlefronts giving Allied commanders the impression that there were several times as many Zeros as actually existed.

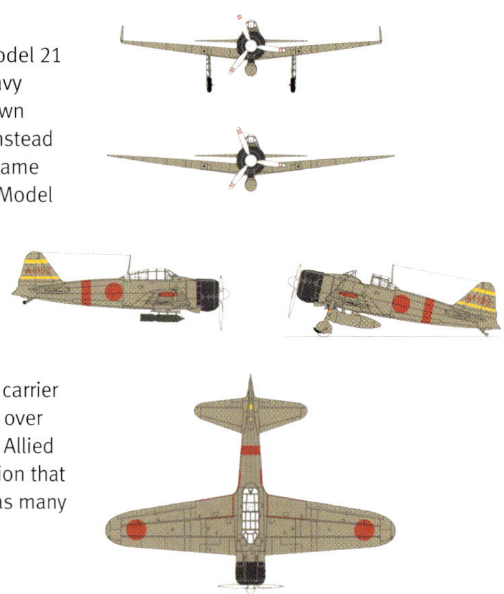

Mitsubishi A5M2b
Mitsubishi A5M2b or Navy Type 96 carrier borne fighter was an all-metal monoplane that came into service in 1936. The type was used extensively during the Second Sino-Japanese War. A total of 1096 examples were built, and during series production several changes to armaments were made because of battle experience in China.

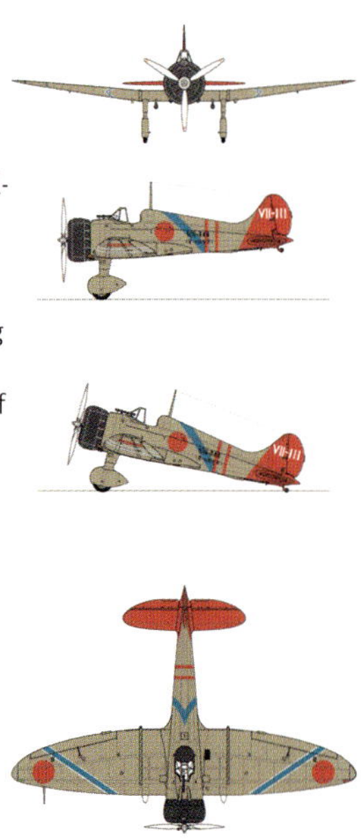

Nakajima B5N2 Kate
The Nakajima B5N2 or Type 97 Carrier Bomber (Allied code name 'Kate') was the Imperial Navy's standard torpedo bomber. The initial model B5N1 first saw action in the Second Sino-Japanese War in 1938 and the problems with an underpowered engine and lack of crew protection were identified. These issues were addressed in the next model, the B5N2 and the aircraft was central in the attack on Pearl Harbor. One of the B5N2s carried Fuchida Mitsuo, the commander of the attack. B5N2 torpedo bombers were credited with the sinking of the American battleships *Arizona, West Virginia, California, Oklahoma* and *Utah.*

Service History

The ships' first operational experiences were during the second Sino-Japanese War after the Japanese invasion of Manchuria that installed the deposed Qing Emperor Puyi as a Japanese puppet and encouraged Japanese encroachments into the now Republic of China. On 7 July 1936, a sham incident at the Lukouchiao Bridge (Marco Polo Bridge) over a 'lost' Japanese soldier led to demands on the Chinese for searches; his non-return was used as a pretext for war. The ensuing war was

Japanese carriers enroute to Pearl Harbor. The carrier *Zuikaku* is at right. The photo is a frame from a motion picture film taken from the carrier *Akagi* found on Kiska in 1943. *(US Naval History and Heritage Command)*

TABLE 2. SYNOPSIS OF SIGNIFICANT EVENTS IN *AKAGI* AND *KAGA*'S JOINT CHRONOLOGY

Imperial Year	Event
Taisho 11	5 February 1922, Washington Treaty orders the halt of the *Kaga* and *Amagi* class battlecruisers.
Taisho 12	1 September 1923, *Amagi* damaged by the Great Kanto Earthquake.
	19 November 1923 *Akagi* and *Kaga* ordered to be completed as aircraft carriers.
Taisho 13	2 September 1924, *Kaga*'s conversion into an aircraft carrier begins.
Taisho 14	12 February 1925, *Tosa* used as a target ship and sunk.
	22 April 1925, aircraft carrier *Akagi* launched.
Showa 2	25 March 1927, aircraft carrier *Akagi* completed, fitting out completed by November of the following year.
Showa 3	31 March 1928 *Kaga* commissioned.
Showa 7	28 January 1932, First Shanghai Incident; 5 February 1932, *Kaga* loses first aircraft; 22 February 1932, *Kaga*'s carrier-based aircraft achieves first kill.
Showa 9	25 June 1934, *Kaga* begins reconstruction at Sasebo Harbour.
Showa 10	25 June 1935, refurbishment of *Kaga* completed.
	24 October 1935, *Akagi* begins reconstruction at Sasebo Harbour.
Showa 12	7 July 1937, Second Sino-Japanese war begins.
	19 September 1937, *Kaga*'s aircraft begin bombing campaign against Shanghai.
	22 September 1937, *Kaga*'s air group, in cooperation with the 2nd Combined Air Group sink the Chinese Navy ships *Pinghai* and *Ninghai*.
	5 November 1937, *Kaga* supports Hangzhou landings; 13 November 1937, *Kaga* supports Baekje landing.
Showa 14	January 1939, *Akagi* supports operations in Southern China.
Showa 16	10 April 1941, First Mobile Fleet is formed.
	26 November 1941, First Mobile Fleet departs Tanuki Bay, Etorofu Island, bound for Hawaii.
Showa 17	8 December 1941*, Pearl Harbor attack; 23 December 1941, First Mobile Fleet (excluding the 2nd Carrier Division) returns to Kure.
	20 January 1942, First Mobile Fleet supports operation to capture Rabaul and Kavieng.
	8 February 1942, *Kaga* is damaged after hitting a reef in Palau.
	19 February 1942. Aircraft of First Mobile Fleet bomb Port Darwin.
	1 March 1942, First Mobile Fleet sinks the destroyer USS *Edsall*.
	5 March 1942, First Mobile Fleet launches an air raid on Cilicap, Java.
	11 March 11, 1942, *Kaga* returns to the Japanese mainland from Stirling Bay.
	5 April 1942, First Mobile Fleet (excluding *Kaga*) launches air raid on Colombo, Sri Lanka (then Ceylon), and sinking of HM cruisers *Dorsetshire* and *Cornwall*.
	9 April 1942, First Mobile Fleet (excluding *Kaga*) launches an air raid on Trincomalee, Ceylon, sinking HM carrier *Hermes*.
	27 May 1942, (excluding the 5th Carrier Squadron) departs Kure for attack on Midway.
	5 June 1942, *Akagi* heavily damaged and *Kaga* sunk by American carrier aircraft.
	6 June 1942, *Akagi* scuttled by torpedoes.
	10 August 1942, *Kaga* stricken from the navy register
	25 September 1942, *Akagi* stricken from the navy register.

Note: Compiled from *Complete guide to the carriers Akagi, Kaga, Shokaku and Zuikaku*, Icarus Publishing, Tokyo 2021.
* Dates provided are from the Japanese calendar.

A Mitsubishi A5M2 (tail code A1-108) takes off from the aircraft carrier *Akagi*, on its way to attack Pearl Harbor during the morning of 7 December 1941. The original of this image is reversed so it has been flipped for publication. *(US Naval History and Heritage Command)*

significant in that the Japanese experiences in China helped further develop the IJN's carrier doctrine. One lesson learned was the importance of concentration and mass in projecting naval air power ashore. As a result, in April 1941, the IJN formed the First Air Fleet to combine all its fleet carriers under a single command. On 10 April, *Akagi* and *Kaga* were assigned to the First Carrier Division. *Akagi* was designated as the flagship for the First Air Fleet, a role the ship retained until her sinking fourteen months later. The Second Division comprised the carriers *Hiryū* and *Sōryū*, and Fifth was *Shōkaku* and *Zuikaku*. The First Air Fleet was *not* considered the navy's primary strategic striking force, rather was an integral component of the *Decisive Battle Doctrine* centred on battleships. The navy's doctrine on air strikes combined the air groups of entire carrier divisions for massed attacks as opposed to sending in air groups of individual carriers. A typical air group strike from each carrier would be composed of as many aircraft as could be arrayed at one time on the deck (called a *deck load strike*) with subsequent attack waves consisting of the next deck load of aircraft. As such, First Air Fleet attacks would often consist of at least two massed waves of aircraft.

However, the Japanese remained concerned that concentrating all its carriers into divisions would render them vulnerable

TABLE 1. BATTLE OF MIDWAY: INTERROGATIONS OF JAPANESE OFFICIALS

Interrogation of: Captain Aoki, Taijiro, IJN. Commanding Officer of *Akagi* (CV) at Battle of Midway. He was not a pilot.

Interrogated by: Captain C Shands, USN.

Allied Officers present: Brig Gen G Gardner, USA; Cmdr T H Moorer, USN; Lt Cmdr J A Field, Jr, USNR.

Summary

The *Akagi* was one of four aircraft carriers comprising the Eleventh Air Fleet, in the striking force at the planned occupation of Midway Island, June 1942. The CVs were first attacked about 200 miles from Midway, 2 hours after sunrise, 4 June by many planes carrying torpedoes, all of which were avoided. The first indication of the presence of the United States carriers was the dive-bombing attack which scored two hits on the *Akagi*. The *Akagi* had launched half of her planes to bomb Midway but forty were still being serviced when hit. No more were launched. 200 were lost and 100 wounded, out of a total complement of 1400. On the morning of the 5th a Japanese DD torpedoed and sank the *Akagi*. The *Kaga*, *Soryu*, and *Hiryu* were sunk due to damage inflicted by dive bombers. No other damage was sustained from air attack by ships in the striking force except possible damage to one battleship's superstructure. No planes seen on the 5th or later during retirement.

The loss of the CV's caused plans for the occupation to be abandoned.

TRANSCRIPT

SHANDS: What ships were present in the carrier force at Midway?

AOKI: *Akagi*, *Kaga*, *Hiryu* and *Soryu* (all CVs) *Hiyei* or *Haruna* and *Kirishima* (BB), *Tone* and *Chikuma* (CA), *Nagara* (CL), about ten or twelve destroyers. *Akagi* was in the Eleventh Air Fleet.

SHANDS: What were the other three units?
AOKI: The Grand Fleet was there to act as support, commanded by Admiral Yamamoto.

SHANDS: What was the mission of the Eleventh Air Fleet?
AOKI: Simply to bombard Midway by planes.

SHANDS: What was the mission of the entire fleet?
AOKI: That was to help. Entirely separate from this was the occupation force.

SHANDS: Was the Air Fleet separate from the Grand Fleet?
AOKI: Yes, of course it was under the Grand Fleet, but was a separate force.

SHANDS: During the approach to Midway when did you expect the first air attack?
AOKI: About 500 miles from Midway, but our carriers were first attacked in the morning about two hours after sunrise, about 200 miles from Midway.

SHANDS: What type planes made the first attack?
AOKI: Torpedo planes, then dive bombers. First a great many torpedoes were dropped from planes, then dive bombers hit.

SHANDS: Were any attacks made on the carrier force during the approach by B-17s or PBYs?
AOKI: There were none. Torpedo planes in the morning of attack but no four engine bombers.

SHANDS: Were any planes seen or heard during the approach the 1st, 2nd, and 3rd of June?
AOKI: There was a high fog and the day before the action opened they heard one above the clouds in the daytime.

SHANDS: Was the *Akagi* hit by any four-engined or horizontal bombers?
AOKI: Not once.

SHANDS: Were any ships hit by horizontal bombers?
AOKI: I think all ships were hit by dive bombers.

SHANDS: Did you lose any ships to submarines during approach?
AOKI: No, none at all.

SHANDS: On the day before the main action about 600 miles from Midway, was the formation attacked by long range planes?
AOKI: No.

SHANDS: How was the *Akagi* damaged?
AOKI: Fire; two bombs by dive bombing about two hours after sunrise (one started a fire at after elevator). Planes were loaded up with bombs inside the hangar and caught fire.

SHANDS: Did you see any horizontal bombers over the formation at the time?
AOKI: *Kirishima* was under attack by horizontal bombing. It was not hit. Near misses.

SHANDS: Were the *Akagi*'s planes in the air?
AOKI: About half of them were up attacking Midway. We were servicing others in the hangar, about forty on board. We had high cover of 6 Zero Type fighters in addition.

SHANDS: Was this the first group launched from *Akagi*?
AOKI: This was the first group launched from all the ships.

SHANDS: Were any other planes launched from *Akagi* to attack our carriers?

to all being destroyed at once by concerted enemy air or surface strikes. The divisional fleet carriers were ordered to operate in loose rectangular formations with approximately 7000m separating each carrier that probably did little to enhance survivability. More critical was the limitations of Japanese anti-aircraft fire control systems and that the fleet's combat air patrols consisted of insufficient fighter aircraft for the task coupled with poor radio communications that inhibited effective command and control of the aircraft. The Japanese also lacked radar, and the carriers' escorting warships were not trained or deployed to provide close anti-aircraft support that would eventually doom *Akagi* and *Kaga*.

The renewal of hostilities with the Republic of China found *Akagi* undergoing modernization and *Kaga* in home waters. *Kaga* was deployed escorting ships taking army reinforcements from Japan to China. With *Hōshō* and *Ryūjō*, *Kaga* took station in the East China Sea as part of the 3rd Fleet and began supporting Japanese military operations along the coast surrounding Shanghai and further inland on 15 August. On this day *Kaga*'s aircraft fought their first

Type 99 Carrier Bomber (Val) drops a 250kg bomb during the Pearl Harbor attack. *(US National Archives)*

AOKI: There was no second flight from the *Akagi*.

SHANDS: Which type of attack was most feared – horizontal, dive bombing or torpedo?
AOKI: Diving, you can swing away from torpedoes, but the worst is dive-bombing.

SHANDS: Was *Akagi* sunk as a result of those two bomb hits or was she sunk later by Japanese destroyers?
AOKI: It did not sink by bombs. She was sunk by a Japanese destroyer's torpedoes during the next morning. Engines were helpless, fire damage, could not navigate so gave up the ship; many engineers were killed. 200 were lost, 100 were wounded out of 1400 on board.

SHANDS: How many pilots were saved; how many lost?
AOKI: Six pilots were lost. Others landed and were picked up by destroyers.

SHANDS: Why didn't the task force continue to Midway?
AOKI: Too much damage to aircraft carriers, lost control of air.

SHANDS: What other carriers or ships were lost?
AOKI: *Kaga*, *Soryu*, *Hiryu*. No damage to battleships or serious damage to any other ships in our group.

SHANDS: In what other operations was the *Akagi*?
AOKI: Pearl Harbor was the first, she attacked at Ceylon and Trincomalee, next Midway. Midway was the only action in which I was aboard.

SHANDS: Did our aircraft carrier raids on Japan affect the training of pilots during the war?
AOKI: When your planes were attacking, we had to stop training and so lost time besides training planes. However, we didn't suffer much from the loss of training planes.

SHANDS: Had the Navy planned on a war of long duration?
AOKI: They were all talking that it would be long, but nobody hazarded a guess as to duration. As soon as it began, we thought it would be a long war.

SHANDS: About how many planes or pilots did you expect to lose at Midway, that is from anti-aircraft and attack?
AOKI: Because we had suffered so little at Pearl Harbor at the beginning of the war, we thought we would get away with the same thing at Midway. I think that other ships in the task force lost a good many pilots, but as far as my ship was concerned, we got off very easily.

SHANDS: Did you have radar on the *Akagi*?
AOKI: No.

SHANDS: Did any ships at Midway have radar?
AOKI: *Yamato*, *Mutsu* and *Nagato* in the Grand Fleet may have had it. There was no ship at Midway or carrier which had it.

SHANDS: Do you know when they were first installed and first used?
AOKI: I don't know but when I went to the arsenal at Kure, I saw the grids on the *Ise* and *Hyuga:* It was August 1942 after Midway. I supposed that they must have been installed on better ships by then.

SHANDS: While cruising to Midway was radio silence observed?
AOKI: There was radio silence.

SHANDS: Was an interpreter radio guard stood on CW or voice frequency?
AOKI: There was nothing but curiosity, but there was not a real guard.

SHANDS: During passage to Midway, were flight operations conducted or carried out?
AOKI: Training flights for about two days (Weather bad); anti-submarine patrols every day. No combat air patrols.

SHANDS: What number and types of planes were used for anti-submarine patrols?
AOKI: 97 Type attack planes. Four planes were used for anti-submarine patrol, searching out at a distance of about 40,000 meters.

SHANDS: In the operations at night did the carriers form a column?
AOKI: At night it was the same ring formation.

SHANDS: Were the destroyers stationed astern of the carriers in cruising formation?
AOKI: All outside the circle.

SHANDS: When landing and launching planes also?
AOKI: They were 500 or 600 meters astern at time of recovery of planes.

SHANDS: When you launched or recovered planes did all ships turn into the wind or just the carrier that was landing planes?
AOKI: It was all at the same time if it was a long operation. Otherwise in short operation the single carrier maneuvered.

SHANDS: Did it make any difference how far they were from the enemy?
AOKI: It had nothing to do with that distance.

SHANDS: How did the planes find their way back to the ship, did you have radio homing device?
AOKI: Only radio. As soon as the planes made their attack, they were to come back without radio help. Only on request from the pilot would ship send message.

The full transcript is provided at https://www.history.navy.mil/content/history/nhhc/research/library/online-reading-room/title-list-alphabetically/b/battle-of-midway-interrogation-of-japanese-officials.html#2

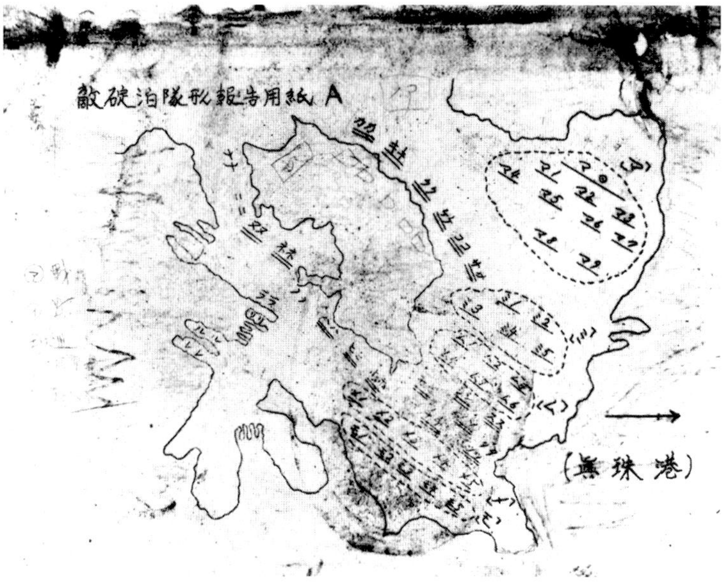

A chart recovered from a Japanese Navy aircraft downed during the Pearl Harbor Operation that identifies ship mooring locations. The code is in the first line of katakana vowel sounds: ア (a) – battleship; イ (i) – aircraft carrier; エ (u) – cruiser; ウ (e) – special service ship; オ (o) – light cruiser. Mooring locations are coded with paired katakana characters or with katakana plus an Arabic numeral, but do not specifically identify the ship types moored there. *(US Naval History and Heritage Command)*

battle when thirteen Aichi D1A1 (Type 94) dive-bombers encountered Chinese Air Force Curtiss A-12 Shrike attack-bombers based at Jianqiao airport (near Hangzhou) preparing for strikes against Japanese positions in Shanghai. Two D1A1s were shot down, a damaged D1A1 returned to *Kaga* with a fatally wounded crewman, whist the D1A1 flight claimed three Shrikes. The next day six Type 90 fighters engaged four Chinese aircraft over Jiangnan, shooting down three without loss. On 17 August twelve of the carrier's bombers attacked Hangzhou without fighter escort and eleven of them were shot down by Chinese fighters. Between 17 August and 7 September, *Kaga*'s fighter pilots claimed to have shot down ten Chinese aircraft without loss, and on 7 September three Type 96 (A5M) fighters escorted six Type 96 (D1A2) bombers and were engaged by three Chinese Hawk IIIs near Lake Tai resulting in two Type 96 bombers downed. Beginning on 15 September, six Type 90 and six Type 96 fighters, eighteen dive bombers, and eighteen torpedo bombers were temporarily deployed to Kunda Airfield near Hangzhou from the ship to support land operations.

THE SECOND WORLD WAR

A great deal has been written about the service history of *Akagi* and *Kaga*, particularly their role in the Indian Ocean, the Hawaii Operation (Pearl Harbor) and their sinking at the Midway Sea Operation. Many well-researched, almost hour by hour accounts of these operations have been published for the interested reader, which is well beyond the scale of the present work. Instead, presented in Table 1 is an abbreviated interrogation of the *Akagi*'s Captain Aoki Tajirō on the Midway Sea Battle (as the Battle of Midway was known to the Japanese) after the war on 9 October 1945, at Tokyo. His answers to the questions clearly show the strength and weaknesses of Japanese naval doctrine described in this monograph.

WRECK SURVEY

In May 1999, the Nauticos Corporation, in partnership with the US Navy, discovered some wreckage from *Kaga* during a survey of a fleet exercise area with the US Navy's SEAMAP acoustic imaging system. Subsequent visits to the wreck showed *Kaga* sitting upright at a depth of about 5400m (18,000ft), buried up to the degaussing wires in the seafloor and with most of her superstructure and flight deck missing. Other artifacts identified included a 15m (50ft) long section of hangar bulkhead, two 25mm anti-aircraft gun tubs, and a landing light array at a depth of 5200m (17,000ft). The wreck of *Akagi* was found two days later at a depth of 5490m (18,011ft); it is sitting upright on its keel and is largely intact despite large amounts of damage to the hull, superstructure and flight deck.

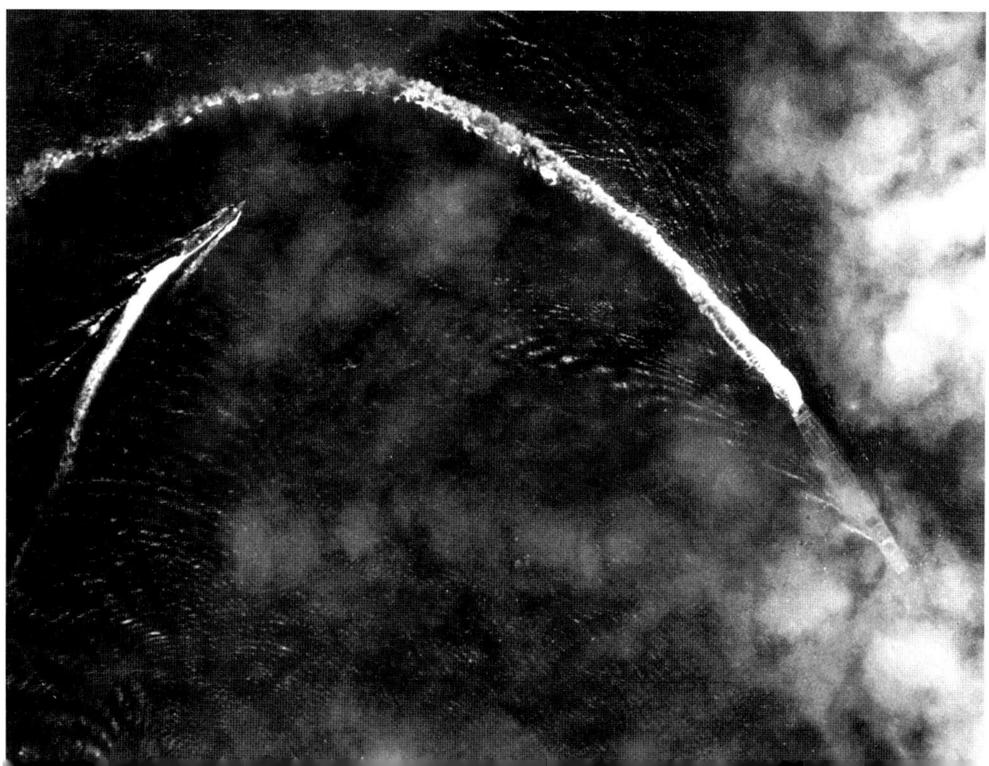

Akagi and a destroyer manoeuvring below thin clouds while under high-level bombing attack by USAAF B-17 bombers, shortly after 8am, 4 June 1942. *(US Naval History and Heritage Command)*

APPEARANCE

Akagi and *Kaga* were painted in the bluish grey called *wartime paint colour* akin to the shade used by the Japan Maritime Self Defence Force (JMSDF) today. The paint was mixed locally at each yard to a standard formula of 15% black, 75% white, 6% brown, and 4% blue. Test mixes by the author using popular hobby paint brands primary colours yield a colour like JMSDF ships, with the best out-of-the bottle match being Tamiya's XF-53 Neutral Grey. Amongst modelmakers and model paint companies there is the general belief that the wartime paint colour varied between shipyards. This may be true because the paints were mixed locally, and the end colour may have varied depending on the purity of the base pigments, additives such as driers, thinner and binders, and the care in which they have been mixed that can alter the final shade. This belief was reinforced by modelmakers who created paint chips from what was touted as paint examples from each shipyard. However, the provenance of the samples has never been revealed but presumably taken from painted naval artefacts from each shipyard. This approach, however, does not consider the ravages of time, weathering or other environmental factors that can alter the paint colour. Moreover, several Imperial navy artefacts held in museums have been restored or repainted. So entrenched is the belief that each shipyard had a characteristic shade that many model paint companies, including Japanese manufacturers, have released so-called 'accurate' paints that reproduce the shade of the paint mix at Kure, Yokosuka, Sasebo, and Maizaru yards. These shades of grey are very similar, and as more paint companies release their versions, the more the shades vary from purportedly the same shipyard!

In contrast, the USN Technical Mission to Japan report (X-32) entitled *Camouflage of Japanese Ships and Naval Installations* dated 22 December 1945, based on the interrogation of Japanese officers at the end of the war, specified that at the outbreak of the war, 'wartime painting gray' was standard across the fleet. As the war progressed, the colour shifted to what was referred to as a lighter 'silver gray', but the

Akagi's bridge and anti-aircraft positions. The photo was taken in November or December 1941 as she sailed towards Pearl Harbor, Hawaii. *(Author's Collection)*

Port quarter view of *Akagi* off Yokosuka in 1927. *(Yamato Museum)*

Close-up view of *Kaga*'s funnel. *(Yamato Museum)*

reason why was not documented. The shift is noted specifically on p9:

> At the beginning of the war all ships, naval and merchant, were painted dark gray. This gray, later lightened to a silver grey, was maintained during the war for combatant ships other than carriers and submarines, naval auxiliaries, merchant ships, and aircraft carriers were camouflaged in colors obtained through experimentation and research.

As such for *Akagi* and *Kaga* whose service was in the early years of the war, one would imagine that the dark wartime painting grey as per the Japanese formula would be appropriate.

The wartime painting colour was applied to the hull above the waterline (no black boot topping), the superstructures, all metal decks, the gun turrets, the topside fittings and the boats. A reddish brown was used on the underwater part of the hull consisting of 20% red, 65% brown, 10% black, and 5% white. It remains unclear if the percentages are by weight or volume. The flight deck (except elevators) was covered with planks of hinoki cypress (*Chamaecyparis obtuse*) and unpainted. The 12cm to 15cm wide planks were laid longitudinally. The aft end of the flight deck was made of steel and covered with non-skid paint. Wooden battens and welded metal strips measuring 200mm by 16mm (treadplate) provided surer footing. Linoleum decks used to dissipate heat were unpainted and the natural colour of the linoleum was described as a red brown but varied in shade.

FLIGHT DECK MARKINGS

Take Off. The most prominent markings on the ships were those on the flight deck used

View of aircraft on *Akagi*'s lower flight deck from a hangar space. *(Yamato Museum)*

View of all three of *Akagi*'s flight decks. What appears to be a Mitsubishi 2MR reconnaissance aircraft is parked on the lower deck. The starboard turret housing twin 20cm guns is on the middle deck. The upper flight deck is interesting for how the wooden planks have been laid and joggled into margin planks. *(Yamato Museum)*

for take-off and landing aircraft. To understand the markings, it is important to know how an aircraft took off and landed. Flying operations were controlled by a Commander or Lieutenant Commander of the Air Branch stationed on the bridge, assisted by two junior landing signal officers. During take-off, the first aircraft was signalled off by a white flag by the Commander of the Air Branch. If this flag continued to be displayed, succeeding aircraft took off without further signal. Intervals of 20 to 30 seconds were normal.

A minimum wind speed of 13 metres per second was necessary for the aircraft to take off so the ship was turned into the wind and her speed increased to 26 knots or maximum speed. A steam vent at the forward end of the bow on the centreline indicated wind direction over the deck. Painted on the front section of the flight deck immediately behind the steam vent was a wind direction indicator. This consisted of six white lines radiating from the centreline at ten-degree intervals. On each side of the centreline was a thinner white line that ran the full length of the flight deck right up to the wind direction indicators. The lightest aircraft, such as biplane fighters, required a run of at least 18 metres on the flight deck, whereas a torpedo plane required more than 100m.

Landing. The ship raised a streamer to half mast signalling '*we are under preparation for landing*', meaning to gain the necessary required wind speed for landing. The ship was turned into the wind and adjusted her speed to obtain a wind speed of 15 metres per second. As the wind speed increased, different signal flags were raised indicating the wind speed attained. When the wind speed requirement was met the ship raised the streamer to the mast head together with other signal flags like black ball, 1 and 5. This meant '*ship is ready*' and an Aldis signal was flashed to the pilot abreast the bridge on the down-wind leg, instructing him to lower his hook and land on. Only in emergency did the landing officer wave off an incoming pilot. On touch-down, one of the junior landing officers controlled taxiing and the other took charge of resetting the arresting wires. Crash barrier operation was controlled by the Commander of the Air Branch. Landing interval rates for fighters was every 25 to 30 seconds, and 40 to 45 seconds for torpedo bombers.

The aft flight deck was also painted with identification marking in katakana script so a pilot could identify his ship. This was ア for **A***kagi* and カ for **Ka***ga*. First developed in 1932, a system of landing guidance lights of four green (called *sight lights*) and two (initially four but later reduced to two) red lights (called *gate lights*) on booms were mounted on the carrier sides. They protruded outward at the flight deck level. The array of green light was placed 10–15m in front of the array of red light. When the aircraft approached the deck at the correct angle for landing (about 6.5° based on the wind speed of 15 metres per second for landing) all six lights are lined up in a

Air operations on *Kaga*. (Yamato Museum)

straight row. If the aircraft was coming into too low the red gate lights would appear above the green sight lights; and if the gate lights appear below the sight lights, the approach angle was too high. The lights were also used as a reference to check for left and right deviations. If the left and right sides are evenly visible, the approach could

The experimental island bridge temporarily mounted forward on the starboard side of *Kaga*'s flight deck. *(Yamato Museum)*

be made without deviations to the left or right. A junior signal officer was present to assist the pilot with red and white flag signals to convey warnings and landing recommendations to the pilot, but the decision to land rested solely with the pilot. For example, white flags told the pilot in a descending aircraft what condition he was in, whereas a red flag indicated that the pilot should abort this landing attempt, go around and try again; a red flag with the letter **H** indicated that the aircraft's tail hook was not lowered.

The aft of the flight deck and wings are painted in red and white stripes to indicate the end of the deck. When the pilot came into land, as soon as he lost sight of the stripes it told him to cut his engine for landing. Pilots were instructed to try for a three-point landing because it shortened the landing distance, and because Japanese aircraft generally had short arrestor hooks. The red and white stripes also provided the pilot with visual clues as to whether his aircraft was sideslipping to the left or right. After landing, the tailhook was quickly raised and the aircraft immediately moved forward to an elevator to be taken below to a hangar. The white circle on the aft flight deck on the aft elevator may have been used as a visual aid the pilot of a landing aircraft could use as an aiming point; however, no description of the circle being used this way appears in any narrative of Japanese landing procedures, so its purpose is unverified. It may have just been for the landing deck crew as an aid to aircraft marshalling. The Japanese landing system was quite effective, with landing crashes on operations averaging only about 3%.

During the Battle of Midway, the *Kaga* and *Akagi* carried a large red *hinomaru* identification marking at the forward end of the flight deck. An order to apply them was issued on 24 May 1942, stating that it should be painted forward with a radius of 10m and the edge around it should be painted white, about 1m broad. This order was followed by *Kaga*, but *Akagi's* officers instead opted for a broad white band with a red *hinomaru* akin to the national flag. The reason for this variation is unclear but of the Japanese officers interviewed in the USN Technical Mission to Japan (X-32), Admiral Yamaguchi remarked that when it came to camouflage, plans and research were often misunderstood, and individuals took independent action. There is also some debate about whether *Akagi*'s markings were permanently painted on the flight deck or were a temporary marking painted on canvas laced to the flight deck using the aircraft tie-down points. The reason for this debate was that the marking appears and disappears in photographs of the ship during the same time-period. However, it is just as plausible that the date of the photographs is in error. For the modelmaker, the question is academic because a model will use the kit supplied decal anyways.

Opposite: An aerial view of *Akagi* and the battleship *Nagato*. Both ships have extensive awnings rigged to block out the midday sun's heat and glare. *(Author's Collection)*

Amagi **Class Battlecruiser**

Akagi was laid down as an *Amagi* class battlecruiser. *Amagi*'s hull was irreparably damaged during the Great Kantō earthquake, to be replaced by *Kaga*.

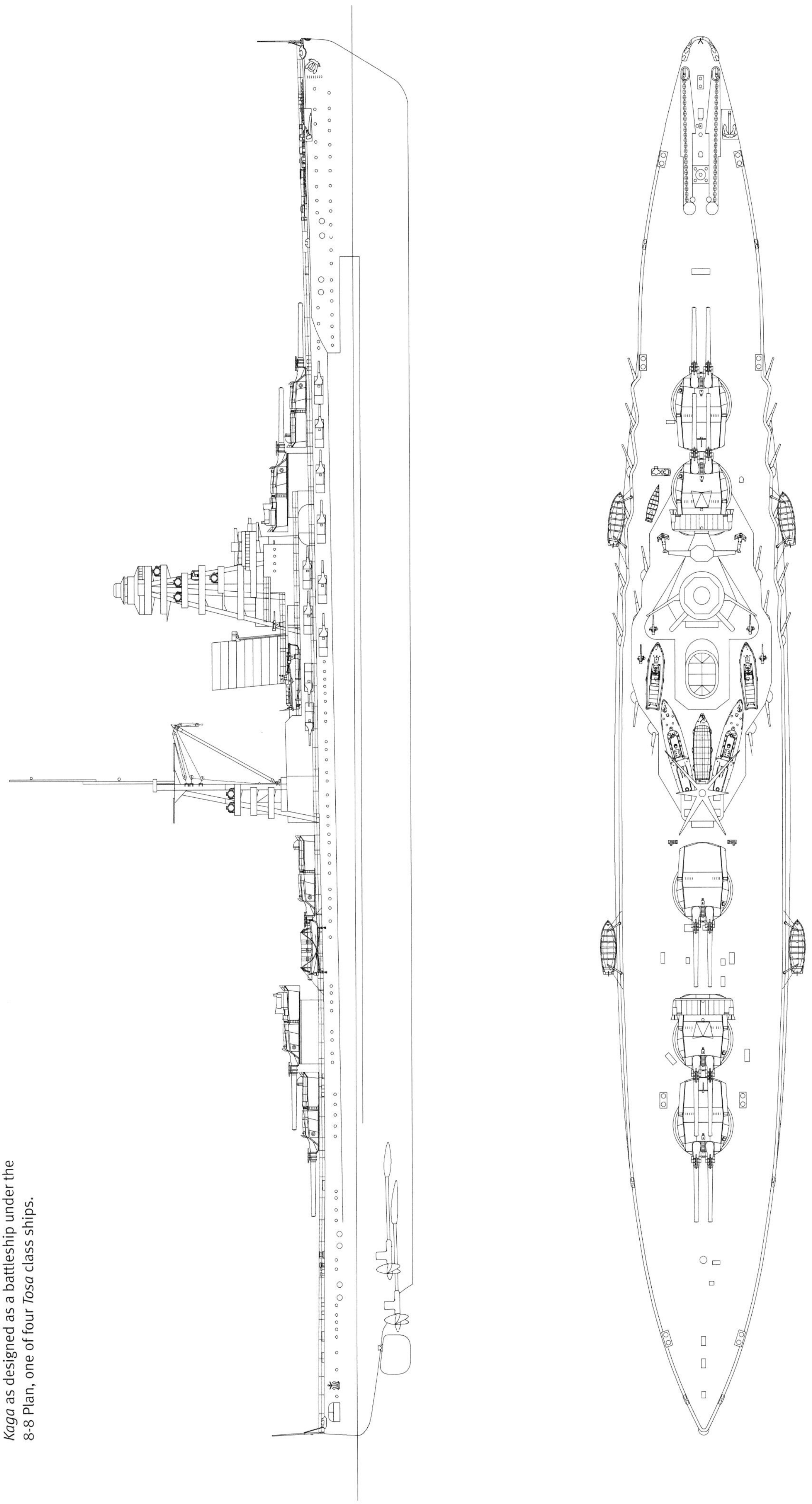

Kaga **Battleship Design**
Kaga as designed as a battleship under the 8-8 Plan, one of four *Tosa* class ships.

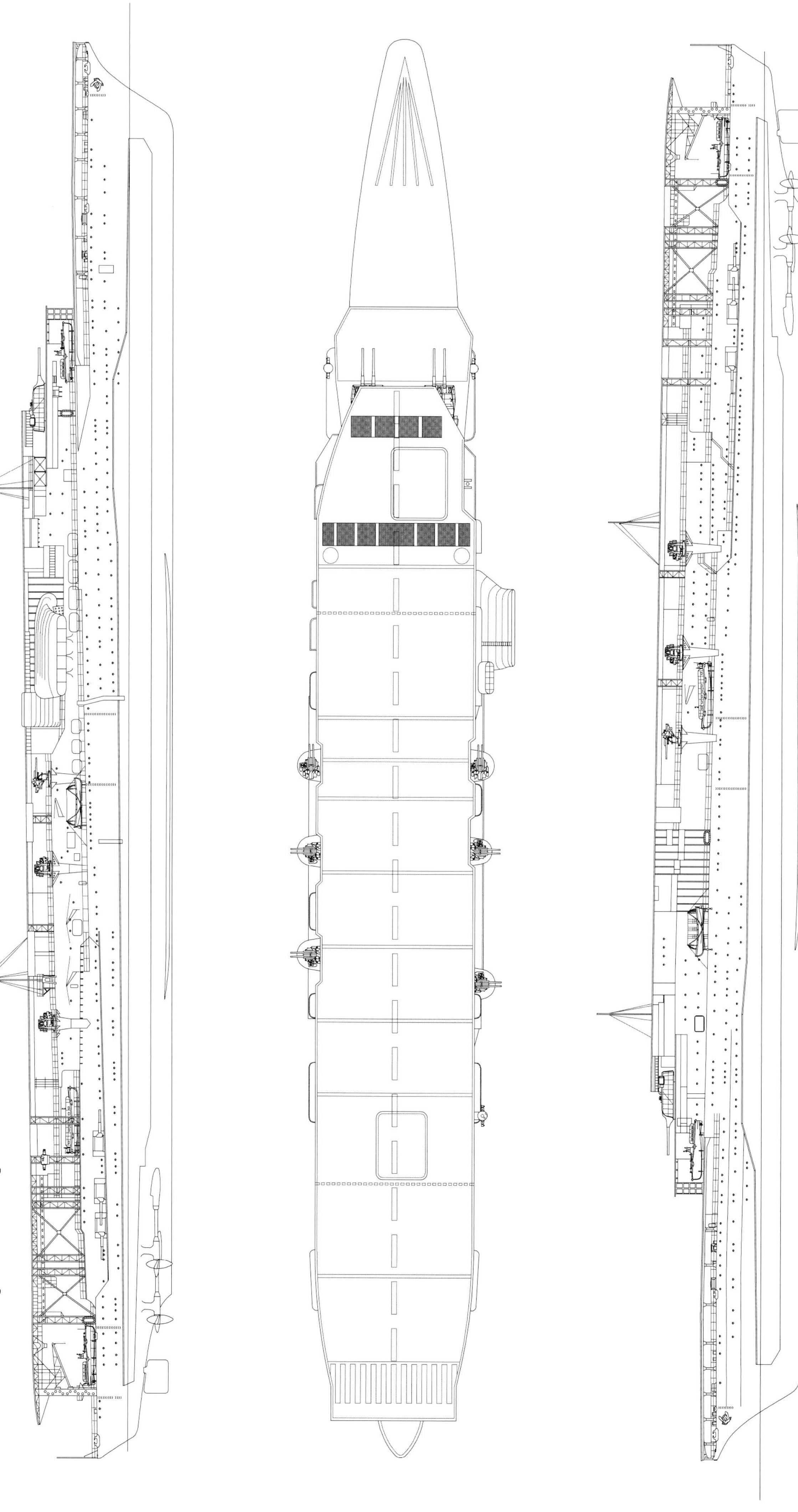

Akagi **1929**

Akagi as completed as a three-decked aircraft carrier in 1929. The middle flight deck was originally designed as a flight deck but converted during construction as a gun deck.

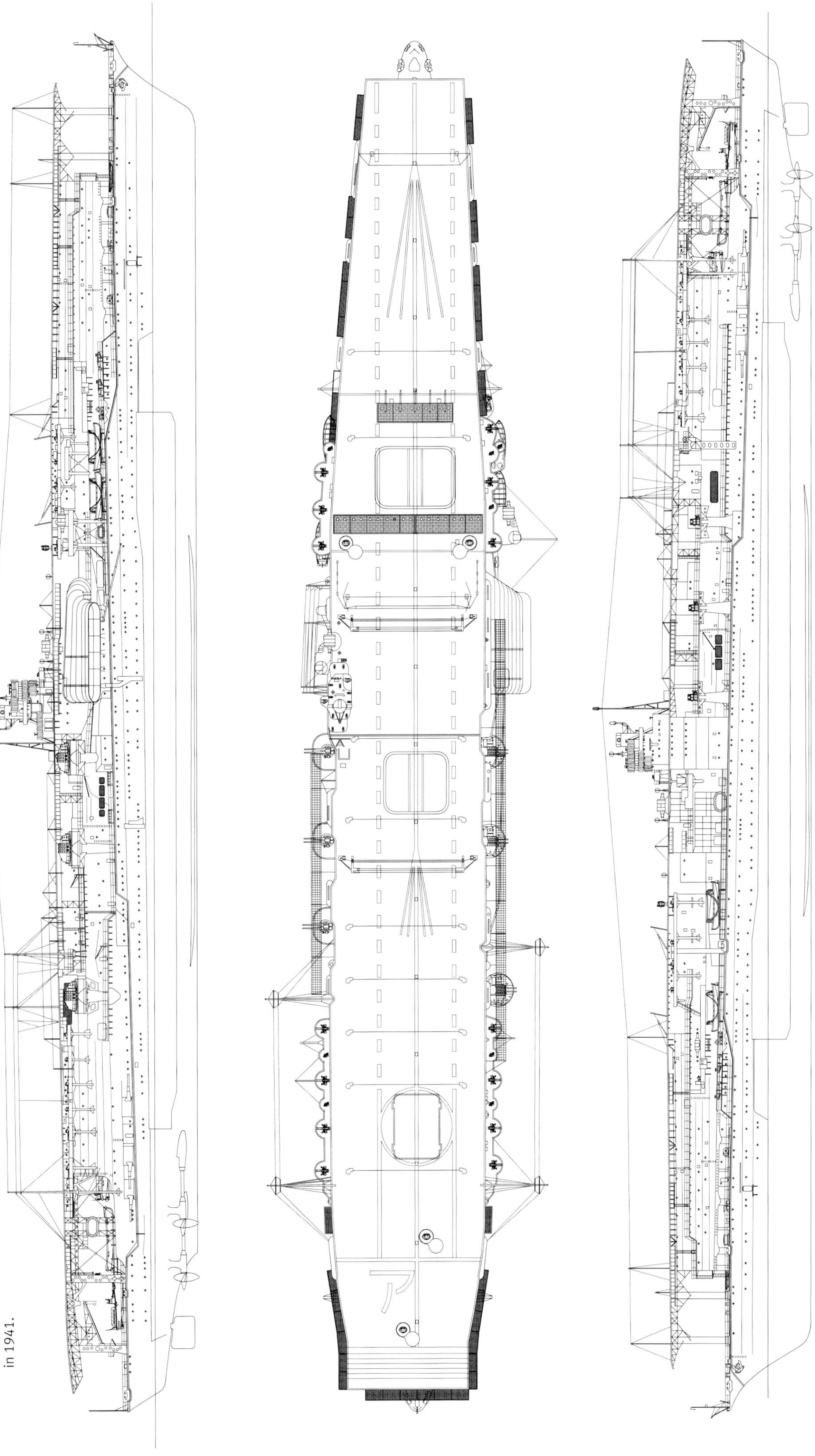

Akagi **1941**
Akagi's appearance in 1941.

Kaga 1929

Kaga's appearance in 1929. The extent of her huge funnel uptakes down both sides of the ship is evident here and one can only imagine the heat the trunking emitted to the crew's cabins that ran alongside them. The middle deck, like *Akagi* was converted to a gun deck, and the ship's bridge located there just under the upper flight deck.

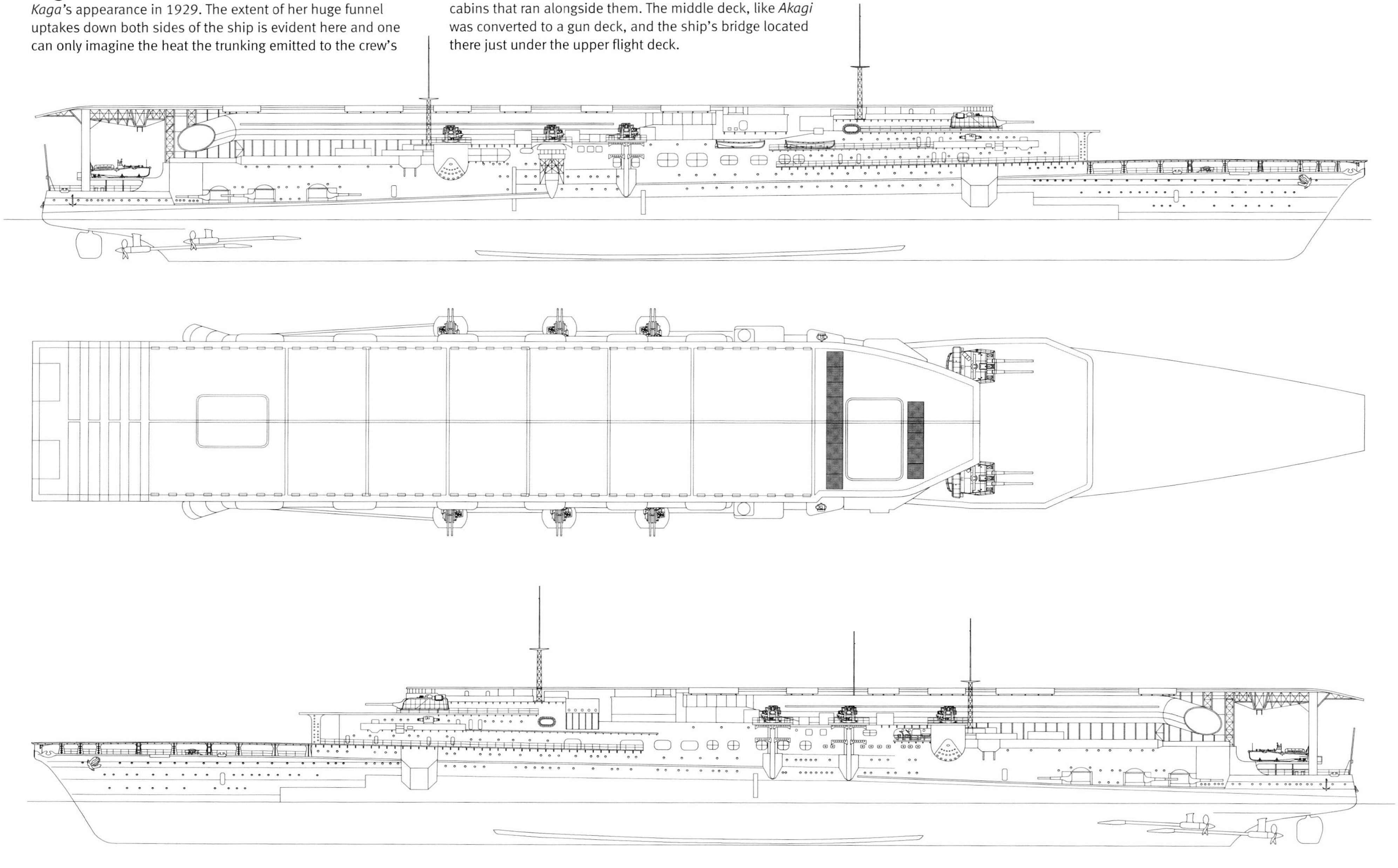

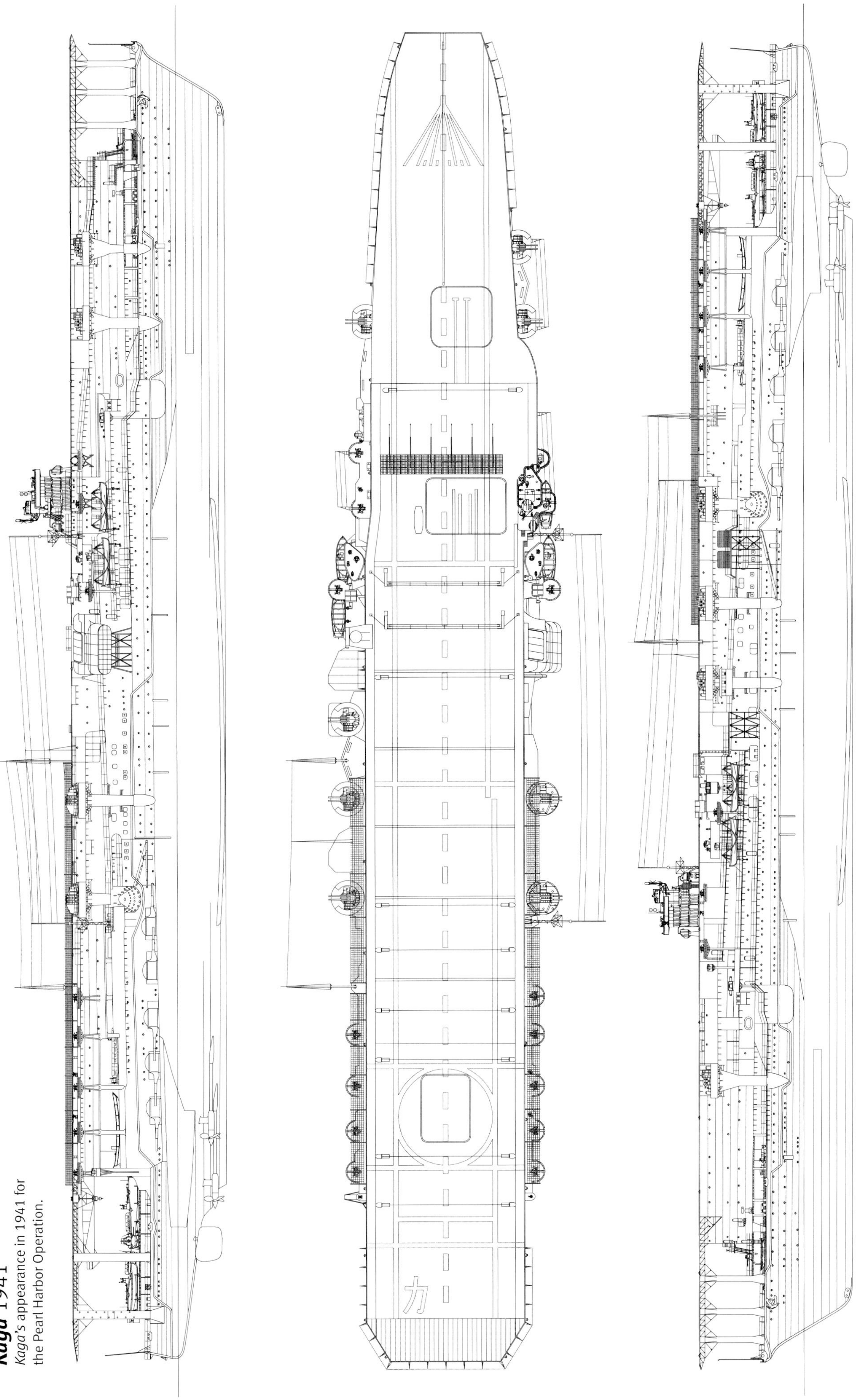

***Kaga* 1941**
Kaga's appearance in 1941 for the Pearl Harbor Operation.

Selected References

BIBLIOGRAPHY

Anon (2021). *Complete guide to the carriers Akagi, Kaga, Shokaku and Zuikaku.* Tokyo: Icarus Publishing.

Australian Association for Maritime History (1980). 'British Assistance to the Japanese Navy during the Russo-Japanese War of 1904–5', *The Great Circle* 2 (1), April 1980, 44–54. Armidale: Australian Association for Maritime History.

Beasley, W G (1972). *The Meiji Restoration.* Stanford: Stanford University Press.

Best, A (2022). *Relations with Japan, 1852–2017: An Overview, British Foreign Secretaries and Japan, 1850–1990.* Amsterdam: Amsterdam University Press.

Campbell, J (1985). *Naval Weapons of World War Two.* Annapolis, Maryland: Naval Institute Press.

Driscoll, M W (2020). *The Whites are Enemies of Heaven: Climate Caucasianism and Asian Ecological Protection.* Durham: Duke University Press.

Evans, D & Peattie, M R (1997). *Kaigun: Strategy, Tactics, and Technology in the Imperial Japanese Navy, 1887–1941.* Annapolis, Maryland: Naval Institute Press.

Hacker, B C (1977). 'The Weapons of the West: Military Technology and Modernization in 19th-Century China and Japan', *Technology and Culture* 18 (1): 53–54.

Hyde, A H (1989). *Scraps of paper: the disarmament treaties between the world wars.* Lincoln, Nebraska: Media Pub.

Howarth, S (1983). *The Fighting Ships of the Rising Sun.* Atheneum: New York.

Kitahara, M (1986). 'Commodore Perry and the Japanese: A Study in the Dramaturgy of Power', *Symbolic Interaction* 9 (1): 53-65.

Koike, S (2006). *The Russo-Japanese War and the system of SHIMOSE gunpowder.* Takasaki City University of Economics: 1, 49.

Lengerer, H (1982). '*Akagi & Kaga*', in Roberts, John (ed). *Warship VI.* London: Conway Maritime Press.

Mahan, A T (1890). *The Influence of Sea Power upon History, 1660–1783.* Boston: Little, Brown and Co.

Mahan, A T (1892). *The Influence of Sea Power Upon the French Revolution and Empire, 1793–1812.* Boston: Little, Brown and Co.

Marston, D & Willmott, E (2005). 'After Midway: Japanese Naval Strategy 1942-45', in Marston, D (ed). *The Pacific War Companion.* New York, NY: Osprey Publishing.

Marston, D & Kotani, K (2005). 'Pearl Harbor: Japanese planning and command structure', in Marston, D (ed). *The Pacific War Companion.* New York, NY: Osprey Publishing.

Peattie, M R (2007). *Sunburst: The Rise of Japanese Naval Air Power, 1909–1941.* Annapolis, Maryland: Naval Institute Press.

Paine, S C M (2017). *The Japanese Empire: Grand Strategy from the Meiji Restoration to the Pacific War.* Cambridge & New York: Cambridge University Press.

Perry, Matthew Calbraith (1856). *Narrative of the expedition of an American Squadron to the China Seas and Japan, 1856.* New York: D Appleton and Company. Digitized by University of Hong Kong Libraries, Digital Initiatives, 'China Through Western Eyes'.

Prange, G W (1982). *At dawn We Slept.* New York: Penguin.

Sana, T (1975). *Japanese Naval Vessels #2. Akagi and Kaga.* Tokyo: Ushio Publishing.

Schencking, J Charles (2005). *Making Waves: Politics, Propaganda, And the Emergence of The Imperial Japanese Navy, 1868–1922.* Stanford: Stanford University Press.

Sondhaus, L (2001). *Naval Warfare, 1815–1914.* New York: Routledge.

Skulski, J (1988). *The battleship Yamato.* Annapolis, Maryland: Naval Institute Press.

USN Technical Mission to Japan (X-32). *Camouflage of Japanese Ships and Naval Installations,* San Francisco, 22 December 1945.

USN Technical Mission to Japan (A-11). *Aircraft Arrangements and Handling in Japanese Naval Vessels,* San Francisco, January 1946.

MODEL SUPPLIERS

Japanese kits and accessories can be sourced through these Asia-based retailers. These retailers have easy to navigate English language websites, and prices are generally in line with retail prices in Japan.

Plaza Japan – https://www.plazajapan.com/
Hobby Link Japan – https://www.hlj.com/
Lucky Model – https://www.luckymodel.com
Kit Masx – https://kitmasx.com/

Kit Masx produce high quality aircraft canopy masking sets and masks suitable for model ships (*eg*, flight deck markings). If they do not have a set for your project, they can produce one at reasonable cost.

Kaga at sea after modernization circa 1936. Note the effectiveness of the funnel in channelling the exhaust away from the flight deck and the pilot's approach path. *(Yamato Museum)*